Making Rain

Written by
Fred Gorski

and edited by
Dominic Ambrose

Ferrandina Press

New York

Copyright © 2015 Fred Gorski

All rights reserved.

ISBN-13:
978-0-9830568-3-6

This is a memoir of a highly subjective nature. Any resemblance to actual persons, living or dead is purely coincidental.

Cover art and design by Carlo Benalis.

ACKNOWLEDGEMENTS

When I was approached by the editor about writing this book, I thought I wanted it to be a legacy of a survivor and a student of life - with life measured on a one to ten, I feel mine is a nine and it ain't over yet. My goal is to try to give my tools to others in order to help people understand that life is worth living and that it gets better and better. I have been blessed by the god and the goddess in so many ways, I thank them above all. Like any wonderful parents, thanks is what they thrive on.

So many people in my life have not made it into this book. It is a very brief glimpse into my life and I pray that another one can emerge from me soon. Vinny, you lit a candle when things became so dark, showing us love can be given with honorable intentions. Never will I forget those feelings. M & M were there in so many ways to help comfort me and kick my ass. Friends help even when it's painful. Paul, the prodigal son, always a boy at Boysbarn. Joseph, who was a comfort even when saying, "I just do not know what to say to help you." It was the best comfort I ever had because it made me understand that there is only comfort in oneself. Sometimes we need to be uncomfortable, sit with it, think on it and get out of it. All of the Pullificos, for being family to me, you will never know the things you gave me. Auntie Mame, for your wisdom, humor and unyielding self-respect, with no shame in making mistakes, only to learn from them (and I have!) Jerry P. for being the one I first stepped into adult life taking care of and then you doing the same for me. We have traveled a long, loving road and I am proud to still hear from you, my friend. Mistress Pain, you had the gift to help bring me out of the dark places into a colorful new life, a rough, tough angel with steel wings. I bow to you, love. Demi, love is the gift you give of yourself. I needed it and you came. We have helped each other through the rough spots with no blame, guilt or shame, better than all the crap out there. Understand my love for you, it is true.

CONTENTS

Acknowledgments	i
1 Editor's Introduction	1
2 Invocation of Lara	3
3 Ocean Breeze	13
4 Boysbarn	69
5 Rainstorm	139

ILLUSTRATIONS

Fred Gorski, 1966	11
Fred, the Staten Island Lolita	18
Mom at Chesterfield Bar&Grill, 1940	45
Aunty Ralph at the drag ball	57
Fernando, Santurce, PR	98
Fred head shot	107
Fred at the salon	132
Dad at Chesterfield, 1944	145
A Female Fantasy	190

EDITOR'S INTRODUCTION

In essence, all memoirs are the same. They are the same story told in infinitely different ways. The story of the human experience.

Factual accuracy is not the most important element in a memoir, as facts have an annoying tendency to be miscellaneous, misleading or irrelevant. What's most important about a memoir is the truthfulness of the experience, the flawlessness of the human logic that propels the life-story forward. You may find a particular story a bit silly, perverse or chaotic but, somehow, it makes perfect sense to you because you can see yourself there in that world. That is a true story, and that's what makes a good memoir.

However, we crave factual accuracy in a memoir, we want to know that these things really happened. Fred Gorski delivers that as well. If the reader can forgive an occasional lapse of chronology, or a dubious motivation here and there, or some third person story that is set behind a dreamy scrim of sentimentality, he or she will find that Fred tells the carnal story of his life unflinchingly and without coyness or ruse.

Of course, characters appear in altered aspect and name, in order to protect their privacy. There are also other inconveniences, such as the fact that Fred was sexually active from a very early age. The story of his teen years necessarily touches upon instances of sex with other underage boys and with older men. That these sexual relationships felt completely normal to him is basic to his experience, and are reported this way in the memoir. Fred is not attempting to generalize about such encounters, especially the age-abusive kind, as to how they would affect others. The story does not condone or promote such behavior in any way. It does not condone or rebuke any behavior at all, it is simply the story of Fred Gorski, AKA Rain Storm.

Thank you to those who have helped and encouraged, John Adrian, Mark McNease and Paul Sanders at Staten Island LGBT. It has been my honor to work with Fred for many months putting this book together. It was a lot of work, but also very rewarding right from the beginning. There was no problem getting the story out: Fred has the gift of storytelling, the ancient skill that have given us epic stories of adventure and historic beginnings. This story just flowed from Fred in a steady stream, like an epic memorized long ago in some classical past. I have enjoyed hearing these adventures immensely and I hope that the reader will feel the same enjoyment as he reads them, as I have transcribed them in writing.

Thus, a few words about that transcription. Although this is the memoir of one person, multiple personalities animate this story and a chorus of voices recite the words. For this reason, the reader will find quotations and reported speech transcribed in a variety of ways, reflecting the various ways that speech is remembered in a narrative. Different punctuation styles represent speech along a spectrum of literalness: speech that is meant to sound faithfully rendered might be in quotation marks, an inner speech that may or may not have had a spoken component, (I'm like ... and he's thinking ...) might be in italics. Finally, generalized speech, the exact wording of which is not important, may simply be undifferentiated in the body of the text. Voices come and go in Rain's narrative, characters pop up and say things. Thus, quotations are not always faithfully assigned, and the reader may have to take a moment at first reading to tell who is speaking.

Hopefully, this punctuation complexity will convey the exuberance of this life, and will not prove awkward or impede understanding. The same can be said about verb tense continuity, grammatical rules ... these are all ephemeral and multitudinous. So please do not look for consistency of grammar, punctuation, syntax or pronunciation. You won't find them here, ... although you will find a genuine Manhattan-Staten Island lingo, distinct from the more widely-known Brooklyn accent. And in that lingo, you will find an invocation of lives lived without hesitation, a pageant of loved ones great and small and a constant rain of creativity and human wisdom.

That's how you make Rain.

Your amanuensis,

Dominic Ambrose

PART 1
INVOCATION OF LARA

A club named Q opened up in Midland Beach. I knew the place well, it was in the Lincoln Hotel and my father worked there many years earlier as a bartender. In fact, the first bar my parents owned was in Midland Beach two blocks away. So I started takin my Fair Play customers there. I would send them over as soon as their makeovers were done (each makeover took about an hour). Then I would join them myself. This one evening I had sent three clients down there to wait for me. When they were gone, I took off my face cream, took the rollers out of my hair. I did my make-up, my hair, put on my shoes, grabbed my bag and my coat, jumped in the car and drove down to Q to meet them at nine.

And as I'm parkin the car, all of a sudden, boom: invocation.

I'm thinkin, *Now where did this come from, what am I feeling?*

I'm feelin the spirit of a wild girl, of a wild girl...that's all I can say. And as I'm lockin the car, I says,

Oh my God, Lara Quig.

******

She was a girl that was way ahead of her time in Midland Beach. She was probably fifteen years younger than my mother and father. She was seventeen when they had the bar. She hung out with all the boys, she drag raced on the boulevard. Tight toreador pants, she had to be almost six feet tall, bright red hair just flowin down her back, this great lookin woman, hot makeup, big boobs, low cut sweaters, skin tight all the way down, high heels. She would just pick her way across the street, and she'd say,

"How the fuck are you guys. Who's racin tonight?"

She'd get in there and one of the guys would say, "Y'got a hot ass, Lara."

And grab it.

She'd turn around and punch him right in the face, lay him right out,

"Don't you touch my fuckin ass unless I tell you to. If I want you, I'll let you know."

Oh, she was a bad girl.

She had seven brothers and two sisters and she grew up learnin how to fight and take care of herself. Her brothers were all bad boys in the neighborhoods, the Quigs, alway brawlin and fightin in bars. But I think Lara was probably the roughest of all the boys and she could lay a man out with no problem at all.

She was a hot woman, always in the bars, got pregnant without gettin married, would never say who the father was, took care of the baby herself financially. She lived with her mother and father, and gave 'em money all the time. She was a barmaid when she got older, she made good money, drove taxis. She was a woman that stood up for the rights of people who couldn't stand up for themselves.

******

I remember one night when I was very young, bein in the backdoor of Inquest Bar. Inquest was diagonally across the street from my house and my mother used to work there as a barmaid. In the afternoons after school I used to go in with my friends. We would sit at a table and have sodas and chips and snacks and play the jukebox and dance. That was our after school fun.

******

On weekend nights in summertime they would open the back door because there was no air conditioning. The dance floor was right there by the back door at about my shoulder height to the street. It was almost like lookin at a stage. You could see the band and you could watch the people dancin, which I loved to do. So I was out there watchin one night, I was allowed to stay out till about eleven o'clock. All of a sudden, some man comes flyin across the dance floor... and here's Lara on top of him punchin him. I got scared and went home.

My mom was workin that night, so the next morning when I seen my mom I asked her what happened. My mother told me that Lara Quig's sister, who was pregnant and showin, went in the bathroom and there was a girl in the bathroom that said something nasty to her, something nasty about the baby, not knowin who the father was, and *no wonder, you're Lara Quig's sister.* The sister said something back to her and the girl punched Lara Quig's sister in the face.

The sister came out and goes over to Lara.

"What's the matter with your face?"

Lara Quig walked over to the girl and said, "You have somethin to say about my sister, you take it up with me."

The girl said, "Get your fuckin hands off a me!"

Two guys walk up to them and said to Lara, "Leave her alone, she's with me!"

"Don't you tell me what to do. She hit my sister. I'll kick the shit out of you too!"

And she did. She hit the girl once and the girl ran. Then Lara beat up the two guys, wiped the dance floor with them. Nobody would step in and separate them, not the owner, not the bartenders. You had to be out of your mind to separate Lara. No, let her go! When she's done, she's done. She won't kill em. Once they're down, if they pass out, she's not gonna kick them. She used her fists, she didn't kick, she didn't pick up a chair. She used her fists. She got right on that guy and she started punchin him in the face - while he was down, yes, but he wasn't passed out. Lara Quig knew how to fight.

******

When my father found out about me being gay, there was a big to do and I ended up running away to Manhattan. I came back to Staten Island a couple of weeks later. I was eighteen now and I went into this other bar on Father Capodanno Boulevard, the Beach Bar, which was owned by two lesbians, and when I walked in, there was Lara,

"Ah, Fred, come over here!"

I said, Oh shit.

Although she had always been sweet to me and she knew my mother and father so well, I was just a kid and she was this big grown up lady. Now all of a sudden I'm eighteen and I'm in the same bar with Lara havin a drink.

"Fred, come on over here. I wanna talk to you!"

I said to myself, oh shit. What did I do? Am I in trouble? Am I the next one gettin hit?"

"You know, I understand, you're havin some problems with the neighborhood. A lot of people are up in arms about your lifestyle. I just want you to know that whatever you wanna do, is perfectly all right for you. You shouldn't give a fuck for any of them. If they have a problem and they come to you and say somethin about your lifestyle, you tell them, Lara Quig said to take it up with her, and that'll stop anybody from givin you any kind of grief. If you have a problem with anybody, you let me know, kid."

******

She knew my parents very well, they were very close. She always respected my mother, Josephine, my mother being a barmaid, too. She'd be in the bar that night and somebody would say,

"Hey bitch, gimme a beer!"

Lara would go, "What did you call her?"

"What the fuck is it to you?"

"First of all, that's a lady, and you don't talk to a lady like that and you don't talk to anybody like that in front of me."

... and punch the guy in the face or drag him by his hair outside and beat the shit out of him and leave him in the sand.

"You never talk to Josephine like that, that's a lady."

That's the way she was.

She'd be on the dancefloor, she'd be wigglin, she'd be dancin and guys would say,

"Who the fuck is that?"

"Oh, you don't wanna know who that is. Keep away."

"No! She's hot!"

"So you wanna dance?"

"Yeah sure, I'll dance with you."

And they'd grab her ass, and she'd say, "Get your fuckin hands off me, I'll lay you out."

At the end of the night she'd say, "Come on, hump." (She called them hump.)

"Come on, hump. Let's go. You're it for the night."

She'd take 'em to a hotel. That's the way she was, free thinkin woman. Call her a tramp or a slut and she'd beat the shit out of you.

******

There were women in the bar, they were playin the field, they were playin with men for drinks, they were loose women, but they were friends in the bar. Unmarried, couple of children and they were loose. And if all of a sudden some guy they were with started gettin nasty, Lara would walk over and say,

"What's the problem here, Ella, is he botherin you?"

"No, Lara, he's a little drunk."

"Calm down or I'll have to take care of things for you. You be good to her, don't disrespect her. She's still a lady. No matter what you think, she's a lady. If you're lookin to get in and get something, act nice to her. Don't act nasty to her, otherwise you'll have me to deal with."

... and they would say, "I'm sorry Lara, I'll be careful."

Or if they didn't know Lara,

well ....

She would go, "Now you're comin with me."

She'd slap em in the face, bring 'em outside.

"Get the fuck in your car and get outta here. Or I'll beat the shit out of you."

And they would do it, they would get in their car and they would go.

"That's it. You're a little too out of hand now," she'd say. "You come back next time and things'll be okay."

That's the way she was.

******

So there I am, gettin out of the car. I close the car door, put my bag over my shoulder and I'm walking across the street careful in my heels and I'm like,

Oh my God, I can feel the whole spirit of Lara in me,

To the point where I had to walk around the block. Like it was Lara saying

I want to take a walk around the hotel. I wanna smell the sea air, I want to feel Midland Beach underneath my feet, I wanna feel the wind of Midland Beach on my face, I just wanna be around.

I walked around the block and it was a beautiful thing.

Blessed be, Lara, come again anytime you need to.

... and I felt the spirit...just go.

FRED GORSKI

FRED GORSKI

PART 2
OCEAN BREEZE

1. COMING OUT

Happy was one of the girls from the neighborhood, that years later was a hairdresser at Sam's. Her brother Hooky and I ... yeah, Happy and Hooky ... we used to wear the same clothes. We used to get the same shirts and dress up. Who the fuck knew? I didn't realize everybody would say, isn't that kinda odd? What are you boyfriend and girlfriend? *Which one's the girl?* We'd laugh and they'd laugh. He had girlfriends and I had girlfriends. I was fifteen and sixteen and I was a little hottie. All the girls wanted to dance with me, I was a great dancer, I kept myself up, I had the big pompadour like Fabian, and great skin. I was a very good take off on Fabian with the eyebrows. I had the one eyebrow, the unibrow, the tee shirt with cigarettes rolled up there under the sleeve, and the black tight jeans or white jeans in the summertime with boots.

All the girls, oh yeah, Freddie, he's a go getter. He's after all the girls. I never did nothin with them. The most we done is dance and make out, that was about it. It was the boys I had sex with. Most of the boys did the same thing. They were with girls just to be seen with them, to make out with them, but as far as sex goes, they had sex with me, or with each other.

When I was a little boy my mother was the only thing in the world for me. I was a mamma's boy until I hit puberty. I had lots of practice with the boys in the neighborhood before puberty, but I was still a mamma's boy, it was just experimenting and playing as a little boy. I wasn't reaching an orgasm, I didn't have all that testosterone, I didn't have all my parts workin. But then all of a sudden when they started workin, I was like "Oh boy, here we go...!" I started shakin. I was like fuck this, I'm goin out and doin what I wanna do ... but I knew I couldn't tell mommy.

My mother, "What's goin on? I never see you no more! Where you goin?"

"Out!"

"Where?"

"I don't know where. I'll let you know when I come back."

My mother was like, *where's my little mommy's boy?*

"It's over!"

"What happened? You don't sit and watch television with me anymore."

"I'm not gonna sit and watch television with my mother. I'm goin out."

But I was shakin, and something was wrong.

My pediatrician said, "You need to question him. He's got the start of an ulcer, he's a nervous wreck. I don't know what it is, but you need to question him and see what's on his mind."

When she came back and she questioned me, I told her what it was.

I told my mother, "I'm gay."

"Damn!" she said. "I can't believe it."

"Ma, you have friends, you have Ralph. Couldn't you see it?"

"No! I'll find help for you. I'll send you to doctors."

"I don't want help, I don't want doctors. I'm fine the way I am. I've made up my mind, this is what I want to do."

There she was breakin out in tears every time I walked past her, so pretty soon my father was sayin to her.

"Josephine, what the fuck are you cryin about? For two days now you're cryin."

"Nothing! Nothing! I'm just upset! It's a woman thing!"

She didn't want him to know about it.

When my father did find out that I was gay, the shit hit the fan, but that's another story for another day.

Ralph, the male nurse, had a yard that was just behind ours. When they tore down that whole neighborhood in Ocean Breeze to put up the psychiatric center, we all moved up a quarter of a mile further toward Midland Beach. Now our backyards were divided and connected by a white picket fence. He was good friends with my parents and very obviously gay. He was always nice to me. We seen each other every day. I'd say, "What're you doin, Ralph?"

"Oh nothin, I'm just plantin some corn."

"Oh, that's fabulous, lemme see!"

We would talk about general shit but we wouldn't talk about being gay. Then I told Ralph I was gay.

"Oh, I always knew."

"Really?"

"Yeah, it was easy, I figured it ... but what was I gonna say? People in the neighborhood would say things in front of me with your mother there. But I would never say anything. It wasn't my place."

I said to my mother, you need to talk to Ralph.

Ralph tried to help as much as he could.

My pediatrician told her what books to read on it. He said, "Fred doesn't really have a problem, you have the problem. He's not going to change, you're the one that needs to change...you need to change your way of thinking about homosexuality and about him.

Otherwise, he will grow up to be an unstable homosexual rather than a stable homosexual."

Oh my God, I don't want that to happen. Not to my Freddie!
The sun rose and set on her Freddie!

I had been a nervous wreck because it had always been on my mind: being gay and not having the approval of my mother. I missed mommy. Now that all had changed. From that day on, I took the medication that the doctor prescribed ... for a week and I stopped shakin.

My mother brought me in and the doctor talked to me about it and he said, "He's fine. As a matter of fact, look at his hand!" he said to me, "Put out your hand" I put out my hand and I was not shakin at all.

It ended up wonderful for me when I told my mother. So much so that a lot of my friends that were gay would go and ask my mother how can they tell *their* mother? ... and my mother would give them advice on it. And if they did tell them and it ended up a horrible thing, they would talk to my mother about that too.

At that point I was goin out in the neighborhood, I was meeting my sugar daddy, Gags. I wasn't going out to dress, though. When I dressed it was with Bruce and his friend Jackie. They would come over the house and we would dress together there. Bruce and Jackie were five years older than me. Me and Bruce and Jackie used to fool around together, and then we met Joey and then we met Raffy.... And this was just the boys from the neighborhood!

We would have tight pants and big bulky jackets, but instead of wearing the jacket like a man, we'd put it off our shoulders a little bit. We put a kerchief in our pockets and we'd get out of the house and across the highway, and then walk two blocks toward Midland Beach, and then put the kerchief on and walk with a swish. Guys would beep the horn and we would giggle and carry on, or they would stop and back up and we would run, run away from them into the weeds. We got a kick out of doin stuff like that.

We didn't have make-up on, we weren't wearing skirts, but we had kerchiefs on, and we were walking so much like girls that a lot of cars would beep as they would go by. They didn't really stop and go for a real pickup, only because there were three of us. If it was only one guy in a car he wouldn't stop and try to pick up three girls. If we were one, it could have been very dangerous.

We were mimicking, we were bein like girls. That's what the Ocean Breeze girls used to do. They used to go for a walk on the highway and the guys would beep and stop and who would get picked up. Many a girl lost her virginity that way down by the beach.

I used to have parties all the time in the basement. I had all the kids from Midland Beach and Graham Beach and Ocean Breeze, from my school and other people that knew other people. There were always dozens of kids down in my basement on Saturday night playin records and dancin. I used to go next door to the grocery store and I'd buy three or four cases of soda and cold cuts and then I would charge everybody two dollars to come in. We had a bar set up with ice and glasses. This was from when I was twelve, thirteen years old I was havin these parties.

Margo was a friend of mine whom my parents thought I was dating. Her girlfriend Viv used to come over so Junior and I would say that Margo and Viv were our girlfriends, but in actuality it was me and Junior and Margo and Viv.

This went on for about two years. I had so many straight friends from the neighborhood, but I also had other friends that were gay that went to school at New Dorp High School. I started separating my life into gay people and straight people. I had my sweet sixteen party and all my straight friends came and then when they left, all my gay friends came over and we had *that* party. All of a sudden people started seeing too many strange looking gay people.

What are you doin hangin around with so and so, and so and so, and so and so? Then all of a sudden you could see the look on their faces, like *Oh shit, I figured it out ... oh shit, Fred is too!*

When I came out all the way, the whole neighborhood found out about me. People kept away from me. By the time I was seventeen, everybody had ceased comin over. So I got a whole new set of friends that were all gay. Then we used to have parties all the time with all my gay friends.

Every once in a while, my straight friends would see the lights on in the basement and they'd come down.

"Hey, how are ya, come on in.

At that point it was "Have a drink, Have a beer, Have a soda whatever."

They'd look around and they'd be like, "What the fuck is goin on here? Everybody is gay."

"Well, yeah, you know I am."

"Yeah, but I didn't think...."

"If you don't feel comfortable, don't stay."

Most of them would not feel comfortable and they would leave, even if they were gay. Like Bruce and Raffy.

The five of us used to get together, get a six-pack and get a little buzz on and all carry on together, and you were fine with that.

And now that you see people here doin exactly the same thing, not even havin the sex, just gay, you don't feel comfortable.

"No, because everybody'll know."

Then don't let the door hit you on the ass on your way out.

And that was that.

It became very well known that Fred is gay and he's got gay friends and he has gay parties ... and you don't wanna be there.

I'd go into the grocery store to get something and I would see one of my friends, I'd say, hi how're you doin. They'd say good and you? Small talk. There was no more do you wanna go down to the beach? Wanna go for a walk to the...? Wanna hang out?

Uh uh. Uh uh.

All right. Fine.

I seen Mr. Lyman in the store one day. He was the director of the drum corps I used to be in. I said,

"Hi, Mr. Lyman, how are you."

"Fine!" and he turned his back.

I was like, *Ooh, got it. I won't say hello again.* I got the cold shoulder. Like get the fuck away from me, you piece of shit.

I guess he figured that since I was at his house all the time, people could have asked questions about him, like why was Freddie here?

Todd Lyman had been the director of the drum corps and his wife, the color guard director. One daughter was the majorette, and the other was the color guard captain. I was the same age as the majorette, and as a matter of fact, I had dated her. But then when It came up that I was gay I kept my distance. I didn't go anymore. I knew I wasn't welcome by Mr. Lyman.

Hooky and I used to fool around together all the time. He lived right around the corner. Hooky had a girlfriend in the drum corps and I had a girlfriend in the drum corps. He used to sleep over his girlfriend's house and I used to sleep over too. The girlfriend and him would be makin out, or out doin somethin, and then she would go off into her room, and Hooky and I would curl up on the living room floor on the rug, under the covers and we would have sex together, Hooky and I.

He was the same age as me. He used to come over at nighttime, and knock on the back door in my bedroom, yeah, my bedroom had a backdoor, very convenient. He used to come over and tap tap tap on the door and Hooky would come in and we'd fool around and then he'd go right back home again and go to bed.

But when everyone found out about me, he was like, "I can't. I can't."

2. WOMEN OF OCEAN BREEZE

On both sides of the neighborhood there were summer bungalows, but this one area where I lived, was where people lived all year round. A lot of the houses were converted bungalows with kerosene heat. We had four bars in the neighborhood: The Towers, Stoutmeyer's, Rocky's Shamrock Tavern and the Ocean Breeze Lounge. Those four bars did phenomenal during the summer time and in the winter time they sustained themselves.

Come Labor Day, there was a parade, and a fabulous Labor Day block party. Then the day after Labor Day it was like a ghost town. All the summer people left and it was only little Ocean Breeze again. But you still had those four bars with the same neighborhood people in them. It was a tight knit, poor neighborhood where people couldn't go on vacation, they didn't go out to dinner, to the movies. They socialized in the neighborhood. We had four bars and that's were you socialized.

People would say after Labor Day, oh isn't it wonderful? Back to normal again!

This is normal?

Back to normal! Now that all those crazy people from Manhattan, from the Bronx are gone, back to our normal selves!

Oh, my God, real normal.

All the longshoremen and people like that drank at Rocky's Shamrock or the Ocean Breeze Lounge. A lot of them were unmarried and they weren't cheatin on nobody ... and they knew who was loose and who wasn't, who they could deal with, and who they couldn't.

They knew Lara. When Lara came in,

"Lara have a drink with me."

She'd thank them, have the drink.

"Nice to see you. Goodbye."

But if Lara wanted somethin, she'd say,

"You know what, come, take a walk with me."

That was the neighborhood, it wasn't a bad thing to be a loose woman. I was brought up being baby sitted by loose women. By Ella Simms ...and Maggie Munro.

My parents had the apartment above the Shamrock Tavern and Ella Simms lived next door above a store. Ella was a sweetheart and a hell-raiser from Manhattan. Her original husband was in a mental institution for the criminally insane. I don't know what he done, but he would escape from time to time and terrorize Ella. She said he was an extremely brilliant man, and he had to be brilliant because he used to break out like every six months. I remember him breaking out at least five times.

She had about ten kids, a lot by different fathers. The two biggest ones, from the original father, were already out of the house.

The Shamrock Tavern was the neighborhood bar and it was very convenient for my mother and Ella. My mother would be washing the floors in our apartment and she would go downstairs for a beer while the floor was drying, and then she'd go up and she would wash the next floor.

Sometimes Ella would go up there and say, "Do me a favor, bring Freddie in with my kids to watch them while I go downstairs for a couple of beers?"

Ella was a loose lady. She was on welfare and she supported those kids very well and when she didn't have no food in the refrigerator, ... Not that she didn't go to the bar all the time, ... but every once in a while, if the refrigerator was empty, Ella would go downstairs and see if one of the longshoremen were there, She'd see someone, ... Bill Head would be there.

"Hey Bill, how ya doin, come over here and buy me a drink."

They would have two or three drinks together and Bill would make a pass at her, and she'd say, "Look, Bill, that's cool and wonderful, you know, we'll definitely get down to business but I need to go shopping for the kids first. You mind takin me?"

"No, I don't mind," Bill said. "Come on."

And she would go shopping for the kids. At this time there were probably six or seven of them kids, and she would pile up a hundred dollars worth of stuff in the shopping cart and Bill would pay for the shopping and drive her back home. She would tell me to put the groceries away and she'd go back down with Bill. Later on that night Bill would come up, all the kids would be sleeping. Then she would do what she done with Bill and that was what Bill paid for with the groceries.

She had a damn good time, and it wasn't like she was a prostitute saying my price is ... for the evening. She would do that from guy to guy from time to time and everybody knew the deal. There was no guilt and shame and blame afterwards for it.

Unfortunately, a couple of times it ended up in pregnancies. One particular time she went to the doctor.

"I think I'm pregnant."

He said, "No, you're not pregnant, don't worry about it."

She went back like three months later and said, "I'm startin to show. I haven't had my period."

He said, "No. What you have is a slight tumor there. We have to see how it progresses, but it's not a pregnancy."

Three months after that she walked in and she says, "Doc, it's almost seven months now. I know when I'm pregnant, my breasts ... I know when I'm pregnant!"

He says, "No, I'm tellin ya, you're not pregnant!"

A month and a half later, she gave birth to a nine pound tumor.

Ella, blonde hair, buxom, fabulous makeup, always wore fabulous clothes. She was full of life, took care of all those kids, loved them so much it was amazing. Did what she had to do to make sure there was always food on the table, but more than that, there was always love in the house, and even more love left over for a lot of us neighborhood kids.

Same thing, Maggie Munro, nymphomaniac.

The woman physically had something wrong with her, my mother told me later in life. She was always wanting to have sex, it was a physical thing. She could have sixty orgasms a day and not be satisfied. She constantly wanted to have sex. She drank a lot - I assume because it subdued the feeling. She also hung around in bars because that's where she would find a lot of the guys she would hook up with. She came from a family from the beach. A very big Irish Catholic family. She was married, had two children, couldn't keep the marriage together, divorced, took care of the kids by herself. She was a loose woman but respected in the neighborhood by everyone, the married women, their husbands, their children. You were taught to respect people, you were taught not to make fun of Ralph for being gay, and you were taught not to disrespect Maggie or Ella or...

Big Nelle: blonde, robust, easy 200 pounds and six foot.

She would come out maybe once a week. Otherwise, she was a stay at home mom, taking care of the five kids and everything. On a Saturday night she'd come out seven, eight o'clock at night after the kids were fed and put to bed, whatever they had to do, with the oldest daughter takin care of the younger children.

She'd come and raise hell until four o'clock in the morning and then she'd be singin in the street with some guy. She'd be runnin down the beach with them, bangin them, run off to a hotel, come home with her panties in her hand.

Everyone would just laugh about it, and say

Ooh, Big Nelle, she went with so and so last night. Oh, she was so drunk, she kept on liftin up her dress sayin here eat this! Oh, it was terrible!

Sometimes, the next morning the oldest daughter, Muriel, would have to go lookin for her, and after checkin all the bars, she would find her under the boardwalk asleep in the sand, naked with all her clothes all around her. She would scream, "Ma!" Ma!" screamin so you could hear her all along the street.

"Ma! Wake up!"

She would harangue her mother while Nelle put on her bra and her blouse, and then all the way home, screamin at her mother like Muriel was the mother and Nelle was the naughty daughter. Muriel would scold her in that loud voice all the way home until the door slammed closed.

Nelle would come in the next week, and they'd say to her,

"Oh, you were bad!"

"What'd I do? Oh my God, I did it again. Don't let me drink so much, it's not nice."

"Ah, don't worry, you're amongst friends. It was no big deal."

And it wasn't.

Everyone just let loose and had a good time.

But not all the women were loose, drinkin in bars and spreadin their legs. Another lady in Ocean Breeze was Mrs. Haughton. She had six children and when her husband walked out on her, she had to raise them by herself. Her children were older than me and most of them were working. Mrs. Haughton took in Jayjay, Maggie's son, as a boarder. Mrs. Haughton never ever left the house, she had that phobia. She would only go as far as her stoop and that would be to call, "Rochelle! Ruth!" and she had that screechy voice like the wicked witch of the wizard of Oz. She wouldn't even go as far as the sidewalk, never go to a store, never go to a bar, never step off that four foot by four foot stoop, never go down the steps either, never hit the ground. She stayed right there at all times.

Ruth and I became very good friends because she was a lesbian. Being the oldest daughter, she took the place of the mother when the mother started getting fragile. She took care of everybody when the mother couldn't take care of anybody. She never finished school, never got a job. When Lower Ocean Breeze wasn't there any longer, they moved the house four blocks. They jacked the house up onto square beams and dragged it with a tractor through the streets and put it up on cinderblocks, so that water when it flooded would run underneath it.

The mother died and the brothers all went off in different directions and Ruth stayed in the house all by herself. She couldn't afford heat or electric, so she lived by candlelight and she cooked in the backyard over an open fire.

She was about six years older than me, and we hung out together. When I started going to drag balls I would bring her. She was like a sweet simpleton, not educated in the ways of the world. She would always look for a girl, but she had nothing to offer a girl, she couldn't take a girl out to a club, she couldn't take a girl even to a movie. So it would be this one and that one, a quick fling here and there. She baby sat for the Stoutmeyers. If you needed a babysitter, call Ruth. If you needed your house cleaned, call Ruth. Ella would call up and say, "Ruth, my house is horrible, could you work for me for two days?" She'd make some money that way so she could buy some jeans or a pair of penny loafers.

So when it came down to the end of the Breeze and there was no more work for her, and no more houses to clean, she went on welfare. The brothers and sisters sold the house and divided up the money. How far did her share take her? If it took her through a year, she was lucky. Then she was out on the street. That's when she came to live with me here at Boysbarn for about three years. She rode her bicycle all over, forty-five, fifty years old, on a bicycle, she would ride down to her brother's house to baby sit the kids, then she would take her bicycle to ride six miles whatever, back home. She would take her fishing rod and she would go fishing down off the piers. She would catch two or three fish, and she would come home and fry them up and eat them. She was a sweetheart, she wouldn't hurt a fly, she was like the village idiot, carefree. Eventually she died of cancer.

We lived in the lower part of Ocean Breeze until I was about 11 years old. Then when everything was condemned to make way for the South Beach Psychiatric Hospital, the Lower Breeze disappeared. Some people, like my parents, moved to the Upper Breeze, we went a few blocks up, to a house with a basement. Some other people went even further. Ella moved a mile away to Graham Beach. I still walked to her house and me and my friend would play hooky for the day and we would go over to her house and she would say, "Okay, you can stay but you gotta clean while you're here."

She would make us clean the house, do the dishes.

A couple of years after that, Ella had a stroke and she became paralyzed from the arms down. She was in a wheelchair for the rest of her life and her daughter Audrey ended up taking care of her. Audrey was a sweetheart of a girl and beautiful, a cross between Hedy Lamar and Veronica Lake. She married Lara Quig's brother

Harry, a helluva nice guy too. They were newlyweds at that time. They had two kids and Audrey took care of her mother till she died, a good eight or ten years. She waited on her hand and foot, washed her, did everything for her mother. It just goes to show.

People might look at Ella and say *dysfunctional.*

But consider all the love that was in that house and all the love that was returned to her.

Was Ocean Breeze dysfunctional? If somebody was so drunk that they couldn't get home, somebody would carry them home. Somebody would put them in a car, drive them a block or two blocks away, bring them into the house, put them to bed. It may have been totally dysfunctional - but everybody took care of each other.

Except for now and then...when you'd have those people that were like Gilda, the bar owner that told my father that I was a fuckin faggot, and that I sucked dick and he should be real proud of having a faggot for a son. That was pretty nasty. That was not a nice thing to do. But for every one person that said that to my father, probably eight or ten people went to him and said she had no right sayin stuff like that.

My father took it really badly in the beginning. Not for nothing else, my father also knew that Norman Perkins and Peter Fowler who were living in my house, paying for room and board, that they were gay. He knew my friends were gay but he thought I was straight.

Margo, my "girlfriend" was long gone, I wasn't bringin a girl around the house for years, but he was still convinced that I was the man about town, that I had girls all over me ... Because I always did, because I was doing their make up, doing their hair, dancing with them.

Fred's got girls in the house all the time, he's always got three or four girls in the house. He's doin them all, he's havin a ball. He's definitely a gigolo.

No. Just doin their hair and make-up. Different kinda girlfriend.

He had come home one night from a bar he was working at. When you close up the bar, it's your job to clean up, wash all the glasses, put them back where they belong, straighten out the seats, wipe off the bar. In the morning they sweep the floor, put the tables all together and they tend bar. That's the way its done with bartenders, the night bartender has to clean the bar, the day bartender cleans the tables and chairs.

He never drank on duty, my parent would never drink on duty. That's what made them fantastic bartenders and always wanted by everybody on Staten Island. They were considered the best on Staten Island because they never stole and they never drank and their registers were never short. Then at nighttime, he would sit down and he would have two or three drinks while he was cleaning up the bar. Then on the way home, he'd say, you know, I feel like having one more, and he'd stop in - because the bars in the neighborhood would always stay open till four o'clock in the morning - and if they had four or five people drinkin, until six o'clock in the morning. Sure enough, he came home and he seen that the Towers still had their lights on, which was a block away from the house. So he went into the Towers and he said,

"Gilda, gimme a drink."

Gilda gave him a drink and she had a load on, and she gave him some news, too. She decided to let him know all about his faggot son. There they sat and had four or five more drinks which probably really built a fire under him, and then he came home and he started screaming and yelling, which woke me up. My mother crying and pleading. It turned into a very nasty scene.

Why did Gilda do that? It was that old story, of people that are guilty who like to throw shame around to other people. A few years earlier, she had been caught in the back seat of her car with another woman. It was the disgrace of the neighborhood. the two of them were totally naked at 5 o'clock in the mornin. I think they fell asleep after they fooled around. She tried this ... *oh, no we were just drunk, oh no we were this and oh no we were that.*

Gilda, you're not married, you're forty years old, you're in the back seat of a car completely naked with a woman completely naked. Are we that stupid?

It was the big joke of the neighborhood.

So here's this woman, four years later, tellin my father all about me. This bitch was thinkin, if I can make everyone else look bad, I won't look as bad as I really am.

3. STORIES AND DREAMS

My father was an intelligent man and he was a bartender so he dealt with all kinds of people. He was from Manhattan, he tended bar at the Chesterfield Hotel and my mother Josephine checked coats. The Chesterfield Hotel was on Forty-ninth Street in the Theater District. Fats Waller used to come into the nightclub cross dressed with fabulous furs. He would walk in, "How do I look, Josephine?"

"You look fabulous honey."

"Here, take care of this wrap for me."

Then he would go in and have a drink. Nobody would know, though people in the band would know. There were so many people like that at that time. Moms Mabley - when she got off the stage she was Pops Mabley. she had a man's haircut, mens' trousers, button down shirt and vest. She smoked cigars and played poker and always had a girlfriend on her side.

Bartenders see and hear everything in these fancy nightclubs. My father dealt with everything and if it bothered him, he had to smile and serve and say Terrific! Have a good time! He was around artsy people, theater people in the Theater District. And my mother grew up in Hell's Kitchen, right there in Theater District, too. That was their stomping grounds.

My mom was raped when she was thirteen years old, by a man named Russo. She ended up pregnant.

She was only out of the convent a year or two when she got raped. My grandfather had passed away and my grandmother was all alone, from Ireland. She had nobody and nowhere to take care of the little girl, so she put her daughter Josephine in a convent and when she got herself on her feet she took her out of the convent and brought her back to live in Hell's Kitchen, where she got raped at thirteen. My mother was pretty stupid about worldly ways. You usually learn all things like that when you're eleven, twelve, thirteen but she was in the convent.

My mother had a Buster Brown haircut, and was not pretty at all at thirteen, but she had a huge bust. She was very self conscious about it and she used to carry her books in front of her chest, but that body on her was difficult to hide. This guy Russo seen her and thought she was pretty hot - and much older ... He kept making passes at her and she kept on ignoring the guy. He just thought she was some bitch, just playin hard to get. He was nineteen or twenty and he was gettin everything in the neighborhood, this kid, and this bitch, what was she? seventeen or eighteen? ... and she was ignoring him? Meanwhile, she was really just a thirteen year old girl with the body of an eighteen year old.

When my grandmother came home, she seen the blood and she seen my mom and she said, "What happened?" and my mother told her. She also told her who the guy was, and my grandmother went right to his family and said, this is what happened. My daughter was attacked by him in the staircase.

They beat the shit out of him. Then a month or two later, she was sayin, "We got a problem here, my daughter is pregnant."

They were like what do you want to do? Whatever you want to do is fine with us.

My grandmother being the good Irish Catholic said, "She's gotta marry him."

My mother was walkin down the aisle with a belly and she didn't even know where babies came from yet. She was soon to find out, but she didn't know. They got an apartment and my grandmother moved in with them to take care of my mother. Russo started making sexual demands of my grandmother. She said no and she went to the guy's parents again and told them this is what's goin on here, what kind of a kid did you raise?

So he threw my grandmother out, *that's the way you're gonna be, you're out!*

It was the middle of the winter, she had no place to go, so she went from speakeasy to speakeasy. She got a big drunk on, and she ended up catching pneumonia and dying in the hospital.

Russo was very good looking and he had a mouth on him that he could charm anybody out of anything. He could and supposedly did have every woman in the neighborhood, such was the appetite that he had. When my mother's baby was six months old, my mother took her out for a walk in the carriage. In the park she met another lady with a baby. My mother said, "Ooh, what a beautiful baby."

"You really like him?"

"Yeah!"

"He looks a lot like your husband, doesn't he?"

"Yeah, he does."

"He should, because he's his."

A year later my mother got pregnant again. Russo beat her and she had a miscarriage. Six months after that she was out in front of the building and an Italian lady that lived there said, "What's the matter, Josephine? You have marks all-a over you. What's goin on?"

"My husband beats me." and this, and that.

"Oh, that's terrible."

"Yeah, I just don't want to get pregnant again."

"Listen to me. You take-a the sponge and you put the sponge and the sponge will catch everything and you won't get pregnant. And he won't know cause-a it's soft."

She did that but eventually he did find out. He beat the hell out of her and got her pregnant again.

That's when my mother left him. She took my sister and she put her in a convent just like her mother done to her. *I'll get a job. I'll get my own apartment. I'll take care of my daughter, just like my mother did.*

She had an abortion, but she got peritonitis from the procedure, and she went to Welfare Island where they had the hospital for people that are indigent. She was bound to die, but at that point they had this new drug called penicillin, and they used it on her and it saved her life. Supposedly she's in the medical books as one of the first people that penicillin was used on for peritonitis.

Russo came to the hospital with the lawyers and he took custody. My mother was still only seventeen or eighteen years old. They told her that he had custody of the baby and if she wanted to see the baby again, sign these papers. My mother was stupid and she believed people, especially a lawyer. She had nobody, the only relative she had was her mother and she was dead. She signed the papers.

After six months she got out of the hospital, and got a job. She started saving money and got herself on her feet and she met my father. A year or two later my mother and father got married. They were also seeing my sister all the time. She would tell her father and her step-mother that she was goin to her friend's house, and she would go to my mother and father's and stay with them for the weekend.

In the meantime, Russo was molesting my sister, constantly, constantly, whether it be penetration or oral sex, four or five times a week. This went on until she was married. We didn't find this out until long after the man was dead and my sister was married, then she told the story about it.

My sister lived here at Boysbarn for a year or so, after she broke up with her husband. She came to live with my mother. I have the habit of calling people *honey*, I'd say, Whattaya doin, honey?

My sister said, "Please don't call me that."

"Why?"

"Because whenever my father wanted something sexual, he would call me honey. As soon as I heard, honey come over here, or honey come downstairs with me, or honey ... " I knew. So when anybody calls me honey, it just makes my back go up, ... I cringe, it all comes back to me. So don't call me honey."

But I would inevitably, constantly call her honey. She would look at me and I would say, "I'm sorry!"

My sister had a daughter that everybody called Murphy. My niece Murphy was six months younger than me. She was like my sister; we were best friends. We were always in trouble together. Murphy would sneak out her bedroom window, climb down the trellis and sneak into Manhattan from the Bronx. I would come over from Staten Island and we would meet in the Village. She would put this wild makeup on. She was sixteen and she was chubby so she had these big titties. She would do her hair up good and she would make herself look older. She would go into the liquor store and get a pint of liquor and we would go to the Village Gate and order sodas and put the liquor in the soda and listen to the music. She'd sneak back into the house like that again. Every once in a while she'd get caught and she'd get the shit knocked out of her.

When I was a teenager, my sister would come over to Ocean Breeze with her husband and all the kids. We would plead, "Please, leave Murphy for the week. It's summer, she has no school or anything. You have enough to take care of with the other kids. Leave

Murphy here with Freddie, cause Freddie has nobody, and Murphy has nobody her own age."

So they would leave her at my house for the week and we would run the streets. We were terrible. Then later, we would sit at the kitchen table and my mom would tell stories till the sun came up. We would play cards and then we would sit there late at night, bleary eyed, holding our heads up, listenin to the stories ...after story after story.

We loved the stories so much. To this day, I can smell my mother's perfume. I can feel the texture of the blue Formica of the table, with the greenback vinyl seats, and the big nails that were holding the vinyl on. So many amazing stories and they all had a moral to them or something to learn. There was always that thing.

There was one time when my parents were not married yet. She was in a department store somewhere in Manhattan and she met this woman. They were shopping at the same counter. They looked at each other. "Oh, my God, we look exactly alike. That's amazing."

So they exchanged phone numbers and addresses. "We have to get together because this is so bizarre, we're the same height, the same color hair, eyes, skin tone, the same porcelain white skin."

Two or three days later, she called the lady. The phone was disconnected. She went to the address and one of the neighbors said that the lady and her mother moved out overnight. "They were here for years, then all of a sudden one day we saw furniture goin out."

Then my mother remembered her mother tellin her that when she was born, she had a twin sister. But then one of my grandmother's friends stole the child. My grandmother being from Ireland with broken English, did not have the resources to do much and with the police not caring, nothing was ever done. She looked and she searched and she didn't find and that was the end of that.

This was the sister that my mother had lost!

It was almost as if it could have been her imagination. The lady who stole my mother's sister must have stayed in Manhattan also, and twenty years later, the two sisters bump into each other.

Why didn't my mother have any other relatives? Actually, there were a few relatives back when my grandfather passed away. He was an artist and his name was Davis. My grandparents had huge amounts of money because he used to do portraits for people. The patron would choose a pose, and he would sketch her face, and then my grandmother would sit and pose for the body part of the portrait.

It only lasted three or four years. They were bootleggin and he died of bad liquor. He had nothing saved at all, absolutely nothing and my grandmother was left penniless. So my grandmother went out and she had one big party because it was the thing to do when an Irishman dies, - to have a party. She took out every single bit of money that they had in the bank and all the money she could find around the house - tens and twenties stuffed in the dresser drawers or used as book markers in books and she had a party for him the night before the funeral. They laid out the body right there in the apartment. The drunken relatives took the body out of the coffin and sat him up to join in the fun. They sat him at the table, sat him on the couch, put funny hats on him and played practical jokes with passed out drunks. You didn't want to fall asleep because you were liable to wake up an hour later in bed with a corpse!

My mother was very, very young, just a little girl and she remembered all these horrible drunken people. She hated how they got drunk and disorderly, how they swarmed. They were disrespectful, nasty, horrible, Hell's Kitchen low-lifes. She hated it and she never kept up with the family. She lost track of them and that was the end of it.

She was such a storyteller. Murphy and I would sit and listen. Our eyes would be crossed and we would be fallin, tryin to stay awake and the stories just came to life. *Live for your love, don't be afraid to love, and no matter how dark it looks...*

For instance, one particular time, when she got out of the hospital. It was the Depression and she had nothing. She went to a priest in the neighborhood in Hell's Kitchen because she was raised in the convent and she was very religious. She knocked on the rectory door and said, "I just don't know what to do. I left my husband, I was in the hospital, peritonitis. I'm okay now, I want to get a job and get a place to live. Is there any way you can help me out. Is there a shelter or something like that?"

The priest said, "Oh ... sweetheart ... A woman that looks as good as you and has a pair of legs like that, there's no reason why you need any help from anybody in particular. You can get many, many a guy to give you help."

My mother was in shock, *my God, a Catholic priest would say such a thing!* She left and she seen the Salvation Army. She knocked on the door of the Salvation Army. They said, yes?

"I need a bed."

They said come right in! They gave her a cot and in the morning they gave her coffee, the newspaper and the bus fare to go look for a job. She did this everyday till she found a job. She stayed there until she got her first paycheck. They never asked what her name was, what her denomination was, if she was a Catholic or a Jew. Every night she had a bed to sleep in, a shower to take. They gave her clothes to look for a job in. She would buy a bag of apples and that would feed her for a week. They were the cheapest thing you could buy and she would eat two or three apples a day.

Later on she became a hatcheck girl and she met my father.

The man was gorgeous. He dated showgirls, fabulous, gorgeous six-foot showgirls. He seen her in the hatcheck room and he said, "I wanna take you to dinner."

She said, "Sure!"

"You wanna go swimmin tomorrow?"

"Sure!"

"We're seein an awful lot of each other."

"Yeah, we are, aren't we."

"I'm in love with ya."

"What are you in love with me for? You date all these showgirls."

"I don't date any showgirls no more. It's been a week since I dated anyone but you."

People used to look and say *why her?*

The showgirls, especially. *"That's* why we're not seein you? *That's* why you haven't called me? Because of *this*?"

My mother was far from a fabulous, gorgeous showgirl.

You date all of these beautiful showgirls. Why me?

You're far more beautiful than any of them. The beauty in you is completely different from that superficial beauty. I love you, I know what I want. It's you and me.

My father idolized my mother and he went on idolizin her till the day he died. From there on in, she was treated like a queen.

She said *you never, never, never think that there's no hope* ... as Murphy and me struggled to tell where the stories ended and our dreams began.

My parents were together about eight years before I was born. She wanted to have babies but he said let's wait. We're havin a good time, we go rollerskatin, we go swimmin, we go dancin, we go out drinkin together. They were best buddies. They were inseparable, they did everything together.

My father had been happy not to have children and I hated him for that. When he threw me out of the house after he found out about me, I said, "You never wanted children, what do you give a shit if I'm gay or straight? You never really wanted me to begin with."

"You're right! I never did."

"You would have been happier if I was never born."

"You're right! I woulda been."

All my life, growing up he had been like, oh, nice kid, pat me on the head. There was no sittin on his lap or takin me to ballgames, or teachin me how to ride a bike.

"I work nights, I have other things to do, I'm watchin my program right now, don't talk to me, I have to get ready for work, don't bother me."

So I was momma's boy, all the way. She doted over me and *he* hated it, because he wanted all the attention my mother could give. Whenever he came in, I would retreat. He's bigger than me, so I'll go. I can't be alpha so I'll be omega. I retreat into the kitchen, he stays in the living room. He comes into the kitchen, I go into my bedroom. He's out of the kitchen, back in watching television, I go back into the kitchen. We dealt with each other when we had to, we spoke to each other when we had to.

As I got older, I started getting a little more verbal about my animosity. He would eat his food with his mouth open and I would say,

"Do you have to make noise when you eat?"

"Who the hell are you to correct me?"

That was the beginning. Later on when we had the big fight I said, "You think that I'm a horrible person, but you have to understand, I'm exactly what you are. I'm just as ornery, I'm just as pigheaded, I'm just as obnoxious, I'm just as head strong, I'm just as smart, and I'm gonna do exactly what you did."

"The fuckin kid is right. He's his father's son, there's no doubt about it."

My mother used to say, "You're just like your father, that son of a bitch."

Years later, when he moved into my house, we started to become friends. We talked about it and I understood. And when I understood, I had so much compassion for him. I gave up all the animosity. That's when I realized that I'm more like him than I would care to be. I'm obsessive with my passion. I don't want to share my love with somebody else, and if I were straight, I would probably be the same father that he was, which wasn't very good. I would dislike the idea of having children because I wouldn't want to share my wife. I would want my wife for me. *You're mine, I'm yours, and nothing else should come between us, especially children, they're there, but they're going to go away when they're eighteen. Why are you putting me on the side burner for eighteen years?*

He loved the idea of going dancing with my mother, going bowling, going swimming, running away to Atlantic City or Asbury Park for the weekend. She wanted me desperately and she couldn't get pregnant for years. They went to specialists and nobody could help, and finally there was this little old German Jewish doctor in their neighborhood in Manhattan. The doctor talked to her and said, I think you have too much acid in your system. He told her to do something to remove the acid, some kind of a simple thing ... and she got pregnant. He was a five dollar doctor! They spent hundreds of dollars on doctors, and this was a five dollar doctor, a two dollar doctor, whatever. It was cheap! Crazy cheap!

Then all of a sudden I came along. They wanted a whole different life when I was born. My father was still running numbers and bookying and involved with shady organizations as well as bartending. They decided they wanted to come to Staten Island, open up a bar and raise a family.

4. RALPH

Ralph was not Amish, but he was born in Pennsylvania Amish country, Lancaster County. As a child, he was extremely feminine and he loved to sew, knit and crochet. Even at six years old he would watch his mother and pick up a needle and thread. The first thing that he did was he outlined his hand with chalk on a piece of burlap and then he needlepointed the handprint and decorated it with flowers and birds, Pennsylvania Dutch stuff. He still had that piece of burlap when I knew him. He knew he was gay at an early age. and he loved to do very feminine things. His father would shake his head and walk away, and his mother would suck her teeth and say it's not good, but she didn't really put a stop to it.

He also realized early on that he needed to hide some of this stuff. When he was sixteen he and two of his friends from Lancaster who were gay also, started going to the Mummers Parade every year in Philadelphia. They made their costumes at night when everybody was sleeping. They sewed them and hid them under the mattress and then on New Year's Day they wrapped them up and rode in to Philadelphia on the train. They dressed there in their drag. That would be their big thing for the year.

Somehow, the people in the town found out about one of the boys. Maybe they caught him in a barn with another boy, but they found out and they burned his house down. In the early morning when the fire went out, and the neighbors were all there, the boy's family turned around to the boy and said,

"We deserved this for allowing you to live this way, to be what you are, which is an abomination. We deserved this. We have no ill feelings for the town for doing this to us, we have ill feelings for you for being what you are. We should have gotten rid of you one way or the other a long time ago. You're disowned. We don't want to ever see you again."

The boy left, and Ralph never heard word of him again.

Ralph looked and said, *Oh my God, I'm next. So before I get caught, I gotta get outta here because this is no way to live a life.*

So that's what he done. He got outta there and he came to New York.

He lived in Manhattan and did bead work for Mae West. He also went to the opening night of her play on Broadway, *Sex*. At one point she comes onstage and there are four drag queens on stage and she says, "Oh, I'm so fagged out today!" and she plops down on the couch. The show eventually got shut down. Ralph also ran a speakeasy for the mob, a gay cross dressing hangout in the West 40s or the 50s. He ran it with his lover, who was a stand-in for Rudolph Valentino, he looked extremely like Rudolph Valentino. The lover was also a dancer in Vaudeville, he did ballroom dance with his female partner. During their relationship Ralph found out that he was also carrying on an affair with his female dance partner. Ralph said he'd have none of that and the two of them parted their ways. Ralph said *I will never ever have another lover or anyone that will hurt me like that again.* That was the first and last lover that he had.

That's when he went on the road with the carnivals. He joined the circus. He was a hooch coochie dancer for a while. The dancers were mostly gay men in drag, What did it matter, the boss said, as long as they could dance and wiggle their asses? The carnival would come into town, Casper, Wyoming or someplace, and all the men would be excited to see the cooch dancers. They're half naked!

Of course! But it was the half that everybody's got: arms, legs, what have you. You paid a certain amount to see them wiggle and shimmy and do a little Charleston in their veils and tassels and pearls, sexy with their young boyish bodies and everything neatly tucked between their legs. Then you paid a little extra if you wanted to go inside the tent and see them do the rest of their performance ... in their underwear! Bras and panties that didn't reveal much of anything anyway. But that was enough, and the cowboys of Casper had enough to masturbate about for the next six months, till the next circus came to town.

When he could not do the hooch so well, he became the bearded lady. The bearded lady was always a man. It was a hell of a lot easier for a man to stuff a bra and grow a beard than it is for a woman to stuff a bra and grow a beard, so the bearded lady was always a man. So was the fat lady. What lady wants to sit there in her bra and revealing skirt and get laughed at by these rubes? That was a man's job, and when you're that fat, the bra looks pretty good.

It didn't last though, so he came back to New York and went to Bellevue Nursing School. After graduation, he got into Snug Harbor as a registered nurse. He stayed at Snug Harbor for the rest of his working days and retired when he was 65. Sailors Snug Harbor was a hoot. The snuggies were old, retired seamen, a lot of them senile. They were around the world in more ways than one. Ralph was so very effeminate, and they knew what time it was, those old guys. He would be doing the rounds at nighttime,

"Could you rub my back? I'm a little sore."

He'd go, "Okay, I'll rub your back," and the seaman would grab his leg, "Now, stop that you old bastard, you!"

They were always lookin to grab a feel or show themselves to him with their full erections, or as full as they could be. The old sailors loved him.

"I'd go walkin past their beds and they'd flip the covers over and they'd be standin erect. Oh you stop that, put that thing away! Give it a break, haven't you worn that out yet?"

... and he'd walk on. They were lookin to play a little bit, but Ralph thought, *noooo, I don't jeopardize*. Ralph had the old school way of thinking and he was very serious about his medical career.

He came to live in Ocean Breeze, that little Appalachian hollow by the sea. Ralph was the closest thing to a doctor in the neighborhood, so he did home visits on the side, giving injections and nursing for people who couldn't afford a real doctor. Thus he became an accepted member of the community in spite of his flaming queerness.

When Ralph came home from work, even at 2 o'clock in the morning if he had a late shift, he would stop off at one of the bars and have a couple of drinks. He might sit with Sheila, a good friend of my mother's. Her husband left her very early on and she had a young daughter, so she never got involved with another man. She and Ralph would go out drinking together, have dinner together from when they were 35.

Ralph told me, "I would be at the bar with Sheila and Sheila would get up to go to the bathroom and some guy would walk over to me and say, who's the dame you're with?

"It's my friend Sheila."

They knew he was gay and they'd say, "Obviously, you're just friends."

"Yeah."

"Well, what's the chances of me gettin a little piece of Sheila?"

"You ain't got a chance in the world, Sheila is very anti-man. Before she's gonna give you a tumble, you're gonna have to do back flips. I don't think you wanna go that far."

"All right, so get rid of Sheila and come back and maybe you and I can hit it off."

They would hit it off sometimes, or they wouldn't.

If he went to Stoutmeyer's, he would sit with my mother. My mother could only tend bar until midnight because that was the law at the time, women weren't allowed to tend bar after midnight. She'd get off work at Stoutmeyer's and sit on the other side of the bar and have a drink and wait for my father. He would close up his bar a few blocks away at maybe three o'clock and come and join her for a nightcap. My father would come into the bar and walk over to my mother and say, "Hiya, honey," and kiss her on the cheek, and turn around to Ralph, "Hiya, honey," and kiss Ralph on the cheek.

At Stoutmeyer's everybody was married and there were no pickups or stuff like that. Men could go in and they could drink and they could fall off the stool and pass out. They'd be dragged into the kitchen to let 'em sleep it off. The wife would come in and say,

"Where is he?!"

"He's in the back sleepin."

"That son of a bitch didn't come home for dinner. I knew he was in the goddam bar. So I finished doin the dishes, I put the kids to bed and I come down. All right, lemme have a drink!"

She'd be drunk by the time he'd wake up and then he'd have to take care of the woman.

Ralph would be sittin there with my mom and a couple of other people. They'd have six or eight drinks together, and somethin to eat. He would catch somebody's eye at the bar that would be lookin at him a little too long. Ralph knew what time it was, so when it came time to go home, Ralph would say,

"All right, I'm goin home. Goodnight everybody,..."
"Goodnight Nathan!" (to the bar owner),
"Goodnight Barbara!" (to the bar owner's wife),
"Goodnight Frankie!" (to the bartender).
"Goodnight Ralph."
"Goodnight."
"Goodnight."

He'd walk out and he'd walk very, very slowly. It was about four blocks to where he lived at the time. He lived on a very desolate lonely road in Ocean Breeze, all swamps across the street and next to him. He would be walkin down that last dark street and he'd hear:

"Ralph! Ralph!"
He'd turn around.
"Yes?"
"It's me, it's Bill. Wait up. I figured I'd walk ya home."
"Oh, okay."

He had given everybody notice that he was leaving. Then whoever was interested would have enough time to say, oh yeah, it's time for me to go. Yeah. Have a good night. Good night, good night. Then they would walk out like they were goin home, and they'd slip up the block instead.

These guys were married, they weren't gonna get close to Ralph. They knew where to go for a good time and they would come see him maybe once every couple of months. Then they'd go home to the wife and they'd be fine for a couple of months.

Ralph was always like, "I wasn't gonna steal them, I wasn't gonna keep them. I was doin the wife a favor, if nothin else."

Community service, Ralph, the community chest. Dip in and take a little out.

5. DRINKS ALL AROUND

My mother always wore a white uniform, white tie-up oxford shoes, maybe a red handkerchief in the pocket of her uniform and a red apron to match. Or if it was blue or green, with a bow in her hair, with a bun, the whole thing was matchy matchy, but the uniform was all white, always. She insisted upon that uniform.

The younger barmaids? They would be in skin tight jeans, and sweaters. Lara Quig's sweater would be down to there, she would lean over to wash the glasses, and one of the girls would pop out, son of a bitchin tits! ... and she would put it back in again, fuckin tits are always in my way! ... and she would put it back in again. But my mother was already much older than these people. She insisted upon that white uniform, that's what she wanted. She knew it inspired people to respect her, it set her apart from the rest and she didn't look like a tramp.

The drinkers always said, "Josephine may I have a drink?" But with the other ones they would be like,

"Hey bitch, will ya get me another drink?"

"How long do ya hafta wait for a fuckin drink around here?"

But ...

"Josephine, when you have the time?"

"Excuse me, when you have the time can I get another one?"

It was always that way.

Lara would come into the bar and someone would say, "Hey, Lara, how the fuck are you?"

Lara would say, "Watch your mouth, Josephine's behind the bar and she's a lady."

My father always wore dress pants and a shirt and tie and vest. Neither one of them ever drank behind the bar. No such thing.

People would say, "Come on! Lemme buy you a drink."

"No, thank you."

"Please!"

"If you wanna leave a tip, that's fine. I'll have the drink later on."

And the bar owners: "Take the fuckin drink. Have a drink with them, they're buyin. It's more money in my register."

"No. First of all, the register has to stay straight. When you close out that register there's never a mistake in it. Second of all, if I'm working and I'm drunk, I'm gonna overpour. I could fall. I could pass out. What are you gonna do if I pass out?"

"Take over the bar like I do with everybody else."

That's what used to happen. If you're tending bar, you have eight or ten people a night minimal that wanna buy you a drink. That's eight or ten drinks. You get used to it after a while, but so does your liver. That's not good. By the time you're forty-five years old, you got cirrhosis.

Molly owned one bar where my mother worked. She died of cirrhosis of the liver. Maybe she was fifty-five. She'd sit at the bar and they would say, "Give Molly a drink!"

She would say to my mother, "Take the special bottle of scotch, and you put half water in it. You only give that to me, and you underpour it."

She would have forty drinks a night, but they were really only twenty, but that was still twenty drinks.

"Always fill my glass up with ice all the way so it looks like a full glass. Whenever they say have a drink, take whatever's in the glass, throw it out and give me another one."

Molly said in the end, "You know what? I put myself here to make money." Her husband died of cirrhosis of the liver and she died of cirrhosis of the liver. She put herself there by makin money.

You could find my parents three o'clock in the mornin, downstairs from my house. The bar would be closed and the two of them would be playin craps, crouchin on the ground in front of the bar shootin craps, my mother the only woman there with my father and about eight other guys.

I didn't like the idea of my parents drinking. I hated it when they drank. Then they would come home and they would be in the kitchen.

gnannngnaaaa gnaa gnaa!

Talkin about stupid shit, nonsensical bullshit. At eight years old it would keep me awake and I'd lay there and I'd cry. *Why does it have to be like this? Why do I have to listen to this shit? Why do they have to be so stupid when they drink? Why do they have to drink? I don't like this. I don't like anything about it.* But at thirteen I wasn't gonna take no more shit. My mother overheard me speaking to my friends outside the house while she sat at the sewing machine. It was a summer day and the windows were open. My friend said something about oh when my mother gets drunk, I can't stand it she's such a pain in the neck.

I said, "I hate my mother when she gets drunk, I hate her when she drinks."

... and she stopped drinkin. She stopped drinkin.

It wasn't until four or five years later, that we talked about it. We were at my niece Murphy's wedding and they put out the champagne toast and she pushed it over toward me.

I says, "Ma!"

She said, 'You know, I don't drink."

"Yeah, ma. You just stopped all of sudden like that."

She said, "I stopped when I heard you in front of the house saying to your friends I hate my mother when she's drinkin. That's when I stopped. I'll never take another drink again.

"I didn't mean for it to make that kind of an impact on ya. I didn't mean any disrespect."

She said, "I understand completely."

Later on in life I became my mother and father. I drank. Not heavily, but then I found cocaine and when I did cocaine I could drink even more.

I would do two eight balls in a night. An eight ball is about four grams of cocaine. A normal person would do one gram in a night. I would share it with the world but I would do two eight balls in a night and not think twice about it. I was heavily into partying. I would be invited to people's houses that dealt coke, and they would pass the coke around the table constantly for free, but I wanted to buy. To the dealer, I would say, "Gimme a gram or two grams right now."

He'd say, "No, it's for free."

"Give it to me because I am not gonna be able to survive on what you pass around. My habit is such that I need twice as much."

"So take twice...."

no no no no.

Then they'd look at me like I was there only for the cocaine or somethin.

"Please? Please! Sell me two grams. Make some money on it!"

I would go into the bathroom between all the talkin, and I'd snort. I'd do a line and then the conversation would come to a lull and I'd walk into the bathroom again and come out again, and the conversation...

... and I would do another line. Two eight balls a night.

There I was one night four o'clock in the morning at Boysbarn. All my friends were goin home.

I said, "No no no! Stay! Stay! I have more coke! I have more liquor!"

"No, we had enough. What's the matter with you? Don't you ever have enough?"

"No. No. Stay."

Then I sat there alone and I realized my nose was bleedin. I said, oh shit, my nose is bleedin, ... but only one side is bleedin, so I can still get another line up the other side. I threw another line up the other side.

I said shit, I wonder if I should go to the hospital. *Should I drive myself? Or should I call an ambulance? Let me do another line to figure it out.*

I was like what the fuck!

What am I crazy?

I've become my mother and father, only with cocaine. With the drinkin and the stayin up and the nonsense and the foolishness and the insanity. This has to stop.

I don't think I came to that realization by myself. In the AA they talk about your higher spirit. As a pagan I say I have many higher spirits. It could have been my father, it could have been Lara it could have been anyone in the know.

The next day was New Year's Eve and I had two of my friends there and I gave them all the cocaine I had in the house, which was about a good eight-ball.

I said, "Take it. Have a good time. Don't bring it into my house again because I'm not doin it again."

"Oh yeah, just you! Come on. You're the two eight ball a day guy."

I just stopped. I said that's it, not again.

6. LAVINIA TITS

There was a woman that owned the bar on Victory Boulevard called Lavinia's Piano Bar. Her nickname was Lavinia Tits because she had the biggest pair o' knockers that you'd ever seen and she could take two shot glasses and she could balance them on her breasts, walk the whole length of the bar with them filled and put the shots down at the end of the bar for somebody to drink. Well, Lavinia decided she needed a barmaid and Lara applied for the position. Lavinia was a rough and tumble girl too, she was practically married to the mob. Lara was no slouch, either, she knew everybody in the mob and she was well respected by everybody in the mob. So there was no fuckin about who had more power, they were on each other's level.

Lara had been workin for Lavinia a couple of months. Lavinia came in with half a bag on one late afternoon and took money out of the register.

Two or three hours later, she went back into the register to count Lara out and she said, "What the fuck is goin on here, Lara? You're forty-five dollars short in here."

Lara said, "What're you talkin about Lavinia? You came in here and you took money out."

"I put a voucher in for how much money I took out!"

"Look, you come in here and you take money out of your register, and you put a voucher in with half a bag on, and I'm supposed to make good for the money that's missing in there? You call me a thief? If I wanna take your fuckin money, I'll take your money."

Lara opened up the register and she said, "Here, look, cunt!" She took a twenty dollar bill out and she put it down her bra. "Now I took your fuckin twenty dollars. If I want your money I'll take your fuckin money, I didn't steal from you, bitch!"

"You don't talk to me like that! You're fired!"

"I'm fired? Oh, yeah?"

She took Lavinia by the head of her hair, all teased up blonde hair and stuck it in the bar sink.

"I fuckin quit, bitch!"

And she walked out.

That was a normal day. They ended up becoming friends again. It was no big deal. A couple of days later, Lara probably walked in and she probably said you need the fuckin barmaid. I need the money. Lavinia said, Yeah, get to work ... or who knows what. There was no such thing as a grudge being carried, especially by them.

7. LARA'S END

Lara died in a car crash on Hylan Boulevard, in front of St. Dorothy's. She hit the pole. Now, Lara could drive. Lara could drive and they said there was no way in the world that was an accident. There were no skid marks. She hit the pole straight on, doin about seventy-five miles per hour.

Whether she found out she had cancer, who knows. She was a wild woman, full of love and full of laughter and life right up until the end. There were stories toward the end that she was a lesbian and I don't know how she dealt with that.

She had been friendly with a lesbian that I knew. They were girls together, sixteen or seventeen. They went through the same shit together. This girl would say to me, "The two of us would break into a summer bungalow that was closed down for the winter and we'd bring six to eight guys in there and we would fuck all of them, we were terrible, like nymphomaniacs, it was awful! Later on I realized I really wanted women, I didn't love men."

I don't know what one thing had to do with the other, but that girl went her own way and Lara stayed Lara. Lara just stayed on that path of never having a lover, a boyfriend, a steady. It was always a guy here, a guy there, a guy here, a guy there. She hooked up with a gay guy who was into S&M very heavily. He was also a loan shark and in the mob ... and I said, gay. Glen and her became bosom buddies, they hung out together for five or six years until Glen passed away. They would go off to New Orleans together. Everybody figured that she was into S&M also, that she was probably beatin him up, that she was a dominatrix, because she had that whole dominatrix feeling to her. She always looked extremely feminine but always acted very dominant. That feminine look and that masculine dominant attitude.

Later on you can look at it and say, okay maybe she was a lesbian and she just didn't know how to switch over. Maybe so much was expected of her as Lara Quig that she just couldn't give in to it completely. Maybe in the end she fell in love with a woman and she couldn't just not give a shit like she used to when she was young ... that she would have to go around explaining to people, that she would have to change her lifestyle.

She came down that Hylan Boulevard at seventy-five miles per hour and she hit that pole dead on. Maybe she just said, you know what, I'm gettin old. She seen her two older sisters get old, become grandmas, and she didn't want to go in that direction. Maybe.

I actually did her hair and her makeup for the coffin. Her daughter Millie called me up. She says to me, "Freddie, you gotta do me a favor."

I says, "What's the matter?"

"My mother will fuckin haunt me till the day I die. She looks horrible. You gotta come down and do her makeup. They just called me in for the viewing before they put her out tonight. She looks like an old fuckin woman. She'll kill me. She'll kill me."

"No, she can't look that bad..."

"Freddie, I'm tellin ya."

I said, "Don't worry, I'll go down and do it."

I went down, I went, "Oh my God, Millie what did they do to her, she looks awful."

Toward the end Lara always wore a French twist and curls, massive curls, with a big fabulous dip. But they had done her hair up in a little bun.

So Millie says, "Here's one of her hairpieces, you know how to do it."

I stuck it on. It was bright red hair.

They had a pale pink lipstick on her.

"Take that off! She will kill me! She will kill me!"

I did her lips nice and red. I painted her up nicely. I did lots of blush on her, made her look alive again. I did the cats eyes on her and put false lashes on her to make 'em look nice and big, because she always mascaraed her own lashes, ... even while she was driving. Hmmm ... maybe she was just doin her lashes!

Millie looked. She said, "Freddie, not for nothin, but is she fuckin smilin?"

I looked down. I said, "It looks like she is. She's got a grin on her face."

Millie said, "I swear, she's fuckin smilin at us. She's happy, now. She'll be okay."

8. AUNTIE RALPH

My parents moved to Staten Island when I was six months old and I can remember Ralph from when I was eight years old. I loved him. There was nothing odd or unusual about him, he was just a very nice man that treated me nicely. My mother had friends that treated me mean and I didn't like them and I would be mean to them. They would say to my mother, "He's extremely disrespectful."

"Well, I always taught Freddie, if someone is disrespectful to you, you can be disrespectful back. You don't have to be mean to them, but you give respect where you get respect."

"Oh that's ridiculous! A child should be seen and not heard."

"I never brought my son up that way. My son needs to be heard. I want him to ask me questions because he'll never get the answers if he doesn't ask the questions."

And I needed to be seen. Even at that age I would walk into the room and they would say, what's with him? When I was seven years old people started sayin to my mother, "Why does he walk like that?" *He's so girlish.*

My mother used to say, "Because he stands up straight? Because I taught him to keep his shoulders back and his head up? He's doin the right thing, not the wrong thing."

"Yeah, but its too feminine lookin. Why does he, when he stands still, why does he put his hand on his hip like that?"

"I don't know."

"Why does he act like a girl?!"

I'd be, *well I'm not acting like anything.* Then I tried to act like a boy, and it was too hard to act all the time. Whatever I was, I was.

Ralph needed to be seen, too. There would be fifteen of us teenagers sittin in front of the store because that's where we all hung out, in front of the only grocery store in the neighborhood. Ralph would come walkin up for cigarettes and when he came walkin up it would always end with a very swishy kind of a "Hello Boys!"

The boys would giggle.

"All right boys, move aside! Your auntie's comin up!"

He had this growly kind of voice. You'd look at him and say it didn't come from him. It was a feminine growly voice, like Lauren Bacall.

He'd go up the stairs into the store and he'd put his hand on his hip and he'd say, "Hello, Mrs. Reiss, I'd like to have another pack of cigarettes. I know I shouldn't have them, but give 'em to me."

Then he'd come back out. "Is everybody being good today?" and he'd take a puff of his cigarette and hold it. His wrist was extremely loose. He was overly, overly done. "I don't want anybody bad now, because you know I've got that needle!"

... meaning the needle that he gave shots of penicillin and other medicine with.

He would not try to act manly and he would not try to not be seen. He would walk away with his same nonchalant swish and the cigarette held with the two fingers out high. "Have a good day, boys!"

"Okay, Ralph, have a good day."

At that time, to be gay and proud, you had to be half out of your mind. I guess Ralph was half out of his mind, because he didn't try to hide it. He couldn't, so he didn't try.

A soul is like smoke from incense. It all comes from the one incense, whatever you're burning. But the smoke can go to the right, to the left, it can go around, it can go up. You can smell it on one side of the room and the other side of the room at the same time, but that doesn't mean that it's not all coming from the same place and that it isn't the same thing. The soul is so much like that. When we become spirit, the spirit can be in so many places at the same time even though it all comes from the same place. I often wonder if the soul doesn't travel in more than one body, if you can be reincarnated into three or four different people at the same time. That when you meet someone that you feel is a soul mate, someone that you've become very good friends with, I wonder if that is a little piece of one soul in two people and it's just coming back together.

I wondered about Ralph. I wondered if we were one soul in two bodies because he was so drawn to me and I was so drawn to him, not on a lover or a physical plane, but on a mental and spiritual plane. He had so much to teach me, and I learned so much from him that he didn't even teach me. It was almost like I was craving his soul and he was craving mine.

When everything came out in the open about me being gay and my father found out, threw me out and then let me back in, Ralph would come over to the house all the time. My father would be watchin television and I'd call up Ralph and say why don't you come over and play cards with us. Ruth the dyke from down the street was over and my boyfriend Junior was there maybe Norman and Peter, too. Come over, have tea, we'll play cards. I'd go in to my mother and father and say Ralph's comin over to play cards with us, do yous wanna play? My father would say no, sometimes my mother would say yes.

Every once in a while, there would be a drag ball comin up. "Ralph, come to the drag ball with us! Come to the drag ball!"

"All right, I'll go."

He wouldn't dress anymore, so I'd say, "C'mon, dress!"

"No, no, that's over! I'm old!"

"C'mon you could look fabulous! We could make you up!"

Norman would say, "I'll do your wig!"
Peter would say, "I have something you can wear."
I'd say, "I'll do your makeup!"
"No, no, I'll just go with you."

He'd come with a suit and tie on, nice, nice. We would throw a boa on him at the ball and he'd have a big smile on his face.

He was just ageless. He was sixty five, seventy years old and we were in our twenties. Yet, we loved bein with him. There was no age barrier there at all. He brought to the table all of his wisdom from the yesteryears and we brought all that was happening in the world that he didn't participate in any longer.

I would tell Ralph I was hangin out with someone and Ralph would say, "Oh, isn't that so and so's son?"

I'd say, "Yeah! I'm foolin around with him."

And Ralph: "Well, I used to fool around with his dad, too!"

We used to compare stories, and it was funny because so often they were very alike sexually.

He'd go, "Oh my goodness! Is he big?

"No, he's very small."

"Oh, so was his father!

"That's so funny!"

"Did he take a long time?"

"No, he's very fast."

"Oh, so was his father! That's so funny!"

Ralph lived by himself totally, he didn't let anybody come that close to him. He went to oil painting classes, stained glass classes, to sculpturing classes. He did pottery. By himself he would go to the theater, he would take himself out to dinner in Manhattan traveling by bus and boat and subway leaning on his cane. He never missed the San Gennaro feast.

"I like to go there because it's so crowded, you can rub up against people and they never know!"

He kept those who he played with at a distance by picking up on extremely straight guys. He used to always say, "If they don't look like their gonna pick my pocket or cut my throat, I don't wanna play with them. They gotta be shady, nasty personalities. They gotta be ready to beat the shit out of me if I don't do the right thing. Then I'll go with them."

I think that was his way of saying, *if somebody is a little bit nice to me, I might fall in love with them. I don't want that to be.*

Later on, at Eger's nursing home, he asked me to rub his feet. I rubbed his feet and he started cryin.

"What's the matter? Am I hurting you?"

"No, I just realized something that was very important to me. In all the years since my lover left me, I cut myself off from being involved with a lover or even friends, or even my drinking buddy, Sheila. Sheila used to come close to me. I felt myself needing to be with her, wanting to go to the movies, go shopping. I would say to myself, well, let me find out if Sheila wants to go before I go.... *Oh no! I'm depending on Sheila too much, I need to stop seeing Sheila for two or three weeks.*"

"Ralph, that really explains it. Sheila used to say to me, he just cuts me off like he's pissed off at me."

"No, I wasn't pissed off at her."

"Why couldn't you tell her that?"

"Because it's not me. But with you, Fred, I'm askin you to rub my feet. I realize that you have been so close to me in the last couple of years. You've been the only person in 40 years that I've allowed to come that close, that I would miss you when you're not here."

"Wow, that's really heavy."

"I just want you to know that those forty years of me playing that game with myself, not letting people get close to me, it was a big, big mistake. Don't ever be like that, where you cut yourself off from anything or anyone that brings you love and happiness because you're afraid that it may not last forever. It doesn't have to last forever. Don't ever deprive yourself of the love and companionship.

I got hurt and I learned how to cope with it. For forty years it worked for me. Then all of sudden, two weeks before I die, I realize that's not what I was supposed to do."

... and he held on until he learned that lesson. I'm sure that was one of the deep lessons that Ralph needed to know. Where that came from in a prior life, one never knows. Thank the gods he didn't die without realizing that mistake, because he would've come back and he would've done that all over again. Who knows if we were part of one spirit and that I needed to learn that lesson too, because God only knows, I needed to learn that lesson too. It's one of the biggest things that I carry with me in life. Never never never to close the door. Never never never to lie to a lover or to be in a situation where I can't explain, I can't do, I can't be.

On the last day that he was alive, he asked his attendant, please call Fred and tell him to bring me some fresh towels. I came home from the movies and my mother said, "They called from Eger nursing home, Ralph wants fresh towels."

"Fresh towels? Eger Nursing homes, it's one of the most expensive nursing homes on Staten Island. God knows they have enough fresh towels. They have fresh towels to beat the band! I never bring him towels."

"The attendant said that he said it's very important that you please bring him fresh towels."

"All right."

So I jumped in the car and I ran right over there and he was dead. He had just died.

He had called me to bring him fresh towels. He knew that he was ready to go. I wonder that he needed me with him, - him that didn't need anybody, that practiced for so many years to be alone and to be okay with it. But in the end he wanted me with him.

I still miss him and he creeps into my soul every once in a while and gives me a warm hug.

9. GAGS

When I was very young, I was very sexual. When I was seven, a neighbor found me in the back seat of my father's car with his daughter, both of us completely naked, me mounting her. I don't even know if I had an erection, but I did know how the deed was done. It was the talk of the town, a big scandal in the already scandalous town of Ocean Breeze. I also liked to play doctor with all the kids my age ... and I was always the doctor.

And I had a sugar daddy, though that was a bit later on. He was a friend of my parents. The first time I met Gags was when he wanted to take me with his girlfriend and his girlfriend's daughter to a lake out in New Jersey.

"Let me take Freddie with me, so the girl can have company."

My mother said, "Yeah, it's a good idea."

"I don't wanna go with him."

"No. Go with him. It's fun."

"I don't know these people, though."

"Go with him. Go with him."

So I popped into the car and I take a look at Gags and I say hmmm, there's somethin in here that I like.

We get to the park, we go to the lake. The girlfriend and her daughter were up on the sand playing in the sun and Gags and me were swimmin.

So I say, "Open up your legs so I can swim through underneath."

And I grabbed him.

"What're you doin?"

"You know what I'm doin."

He says, "What are you crazy?"

I says, "No, no. C'mon."

Over the years it progressed to a situation where I actually seduced him. He did not seduce me. Let me make myself perfectly clear. I knew what I wanted and I knew this was available. My gaydar was in fine tune, even at that age. By the time I was sixteen we were an item.

He was a merchant seaman. He was a master plumber on a ship going to Germany and Japan. He'd be gone for a month or two at a time and then he would be back in town for two or three weeks and then he'd be out again on another boat. When he was in town he would call me and we would get together.

People always looked. *Gee isn't it wonderful. Poor Gags, bein a merchant seaman, he never found the right woman, he never had children, and he loves to take Freddie out and go to the movies, take him to amusement parks...*

Meanwhile we were goin to the St. George hotel, renting a room. I'd make him get a six-pack, and then I'd get drunk and disorderly and I'd go down to the pool and seduce other guys. I was bad.

We seen each other until I was nineteen or twenty. He stopped going out to sea and he had an apartment in Stapleton. I would go over and see him once every two weeks. I'd spend the afternoon with him. We'd play around and talk and order food in. He was already now sixty at least. Then I got involved with a boyfriend, Frankie and we got our first apartment together. I didn't go to Gag's house for a while because Frankie was very jealous. Then all of a sudden I heard that Gags had passed away. Oh my God, that's awful, terrible. Oh my goodness.

I met somebody that knew him who said to me, "Well, it was so nice because when he got sick for a couple of months, at least he had Patrick to take care of him, to go to the store for him."

"Who's Patrick? Patrick who?"

"Patrick Perez."

"What are you talkin about? No."

"Patrick and him were together for about three years!"

"What do you mean?"

So that meant we overlapped for about two years. But the worst part about it was that Patrick had been my boyfriend and I told him about Gags and I didn't think they ever met, but somehow along the line they did meet.

10. BOOBOO

Things change. One day Gags said to me, "I have somebody over I want you to meet."

So I said, "Yeah, all right, I'll come over."

I go over and here's this boy Booboo. I was about twenty and Booboo was about fifteen. I was like *oh no oh no no no no*. I'm not foolin around with a fifteen year old, I'll end up in jail. No way. I don't wanna know nothin, I ain't doin nothin. And I left.

Three years later, I was with Frankie in a club and this guy comes over and he says, "Don't you remember me?"

"No. Who are you?"

"Booboo!"

"Who? Booboo? Who?"

"We met at Gags' house."

"Oh my God, you were like fifteen."

"Well, I'm like eighteen now."

"Wow. It's nice to see ya."

"Yeah," he says, "now that I'm eighteen, you wanna take a chance?"

"No, get the hell outta here. What're you crazy?"

But I did have a crush on him.

He says, "Come on. I know you want to. You wanted to when I was fifteen ... and you still want to."

No no no.

My friends knew him, and he ended up getting my address. He found out that Frankie was a pizza pie maker and worked nights. He knocked on my door one evening and he said, "C'mon, invite me in."

"All right, come on in."

One thing led to another and there I was cheating on jealous Frankie with Booboo. I confided in one of my friends that I trusted very much, Carlos. I told him I was foolin around with Booboo. Oh that's terrible.

But then Carlos ended up falling for Booboo himself and he decided that he should tell Frankie what I was doin to him. Frankie and I broke up because of that and I ended up getting an apartment with Booboo. Once we got the apartment together Booboo decided to go to hairdressing school. I taught him whatever I could teach him and I got him on his way to being a hairdresser.

Booboo and I were together for about four years. He was very into alcohol and gambling. He would gamble on anything, mostly bingo. He loved bingo. His parents and his sisters would go to bingo and he would go to bingo almost every day. If he was working he would go to night bingo. If he was off that day he would go to day bingo and night bingo. On Saturdays they would go to Philadelphia bingo where they had midnight bingo. They would play bingo till four in the morning. Oh it was insane! He would bet on the horses, go to OTB, and he would drink along the way. It was the wild sexy seventies or eighties when people were doin back rooms, so we were foolin around with other people together. I had just gotten the house, and I began to think, *This is just not, not what I want out of life.*

11. LEON

One night I dropped Booboo off at bingo and I came back to the apartment to pack for our move. I was driving back to pick him up from bingo and I see this boy on the park bench in Tompkinsville. Oh, isn't he cute, sittin up on the back of the bench, with his tight washed out jeans and a white tee shirt on. Woooh, was he cute. My head turned and the boy followed me as I was driving down Bay Street. I made a turn onto Victory Boulevard and I pulled in there.

He came walkin down towards me. *Oh my goodness, look at this! brazen! hussy!*

He came walkin right over to me and he says, "Hi, what's up?"

"Uh, nothin, I'm just, actually I'm lookin to buy a house and I see this house that looks vacant right here ... "

The two house there that are fixed up nice now? They were dilapidated messes at the time.

I said, "They're both horrible, look at them, they look like they're for sale. I wonder."

He says, "I don't know. I don't see a for sale sign."

We looked around and said I don't know.

I said, "Do you wanna...sit in the car?"

"Sure, why not?"

He jumped into the car and he leaned over and kissed me. I just bounced back and I looked at him and said *oh my God*.

He said, "What?"

I said, "Nothin. Nothin."

I was in love. I was in total absolute and complete love. This boy kissed me and I felt like I was comin down a waterfall. I was tumblin tumblin and tumblin. I didn't know what to do.

I said, "How old are you?"

"I'm eighteen."

"Really."

"Well, I'll be eighteen next week."

"All right that's close enough."

He says, "Let's go someplace."

"Actually, I'm waiting for my boyfriend to come out of bingo. Would you be into doin a threesome?"

"Sure, why not?"

So Booboo came out of bingo. Booboo, this is Leon, Leon, Booboo. Hi.

We came back to the apartment and we carried on and it was lovely.

Leon said, "If you wanna meet again…"

So I said, "Booboo goes to bingo every night and I have nothin to do…"

So Leon would come to the apartment and help me pack up stuff and then we would go pick up Booboo and we would fool around. Then we would drive Leon home because he only lived about three minutes away.

This went on for a couple of weeks until Booboo said, "I don't like the way he looks at you and I don't like the way you look at him. I think we need to stop this."

I says, "I don't think so."

He says, "No, I don't like the idea of it. I wanna put an end to this right here and now before it goes any further."

I says, "I don't think so."

He says, "Well, that's the way it is. C'mon, let's go into Manhattan. Let's go to the baths."

"All right, let's stop off at the Market Diner and get somethin to eat first."

We went to the diner and we're eatin, and he's carryin on how I don't want you to see him any longer.

"Booboo, this ain't gonna happen. I'm gonna see him. I don't wanna know nothin!"

"It's either him or me!" Booboo said. "And that's the end of it!"

"All right!"

We came out of the Market Diner and I got into the car and he says, "Unlock the door!"

I put the car in reverse and backed out and pulled away, and I says, *it's either him or you!*

I came home and he took public transportation back home. He says, "I can't believe you!"

I said, "Look, really, it's either him or you? It's definitely him. I'm sorry, there's nothin in this relationship for me. You're in bingo all the time, you're playin OTB, you're drunk and disorderly, I just bought the house and now he's here helpin me pick out wallpaper, he's helpin me paint, he's interested in the yard. You have no interest in anything except drinking, gambling or going out cruising. I don't want this. You asked me to make a decision. I made the decision. It's done."

We moved into the house that would become Boysbarn. From there on in, Booboo and I lived in separate bedrooms and Leon came over whenever he wanted to come over, which was almost every day.

I introduced Leon to Ralph when we were in this relationship for six months.

"Oh, my goodness, he's a young one, you're bad!"

Then Ralph gave his last gift to me, theater tickets and a gift certificate for Mamma Leone's.

It was New Year's Eve. Leon and I went to the Broadway show and we went to Mamma Leone's for dinner, and then we came home. I was in the shower and Leon was in the bedroom when Booboo came home with some guy. Booboo was very drunk and he went in with a knife and he put the knife to Leon's throat and told Leon, "You took away from me somebody and I'm gonna get even with you. Sooner or later I'm gonna end up killin you."

I come out of the bathroom and I say, "What's the matter?"
"Nothin."
"Leon, tell me what happened."
"Booboo just came in and he threatened me. I really feel uncomfortable."

So I went in and said somethin to Booboo and he came out and said somethin nasty to me. He admitted to me that he put the knife to Leon. He said "Yeah, so what? I don't care."

I went to grab him and he slammed the door and locked it. I took the poker from the fireplace and I broke open the door and I grabbed Booboo and I beat the hell out of him, threw him out of the house. I told his boyfriend "I'm really sorry for actin like this, but he really needs to get the hell out of here. If you really care for him, take him someplace. If you don't care for him, get away from him as soon as possible, because the boy is a psycho."

My mother was in the downstairs apartment. She calls out, "What's goin on up there?"

Here's Booboo runnin down the stairs with no clothes on, (cause the two of them were probably in the middle of gettin it on).

"What's goin on?"

"Nothin, ma! Go back to sleep!" and I chased Booboo down the stairs and out the door and I threw the clothes out the window after him. And the guy he brought home looked like, *I don't wanna get involved with this. I'm outta here.*

PART 3
BOYSBARN

12. MEETING NICKIE

    I was about fifteen and I decided I'm not going to dress up today. I'm gonna go for a walk on Seaside Boulevard. *I'll walk down to see my friend Carl,* about a half a mile down in Graham Beach. Carla Cupcake and I met in grammar school and it was very obvious that he was, ... so I brought it right up to him.
    Carl, what's the deal here?
    No, not me!
    Oh stop it, get a grip! C'mon!
    You too?
    Yeah.
    Oh, okay, I am, then.
    So we became very good friends.
    I knew I'd pick up somebody along the way because I was a little Lolita. I'd walk nice and slowly, with just enough of a swish for people to take notice. Sure enough, I was out there about three or four blocks when a car pulled up half a block in front of me and stayed there. I walked very slowly and I got up to the car and he rolled down the window and he said,

"Do you need a ride?"

"Yeah, sure." I jumped right in the car.

"Where you goin?"

"To Graham Beach, maybe twenty blocks from here."

He said, "Those are kinda tight white pants you have on, aren't they?"

"I don't think so. You think they're too tight?"

"Well, they're not *too* tight. But they kinda show everything."

He put his hand on my leg and rubbed it a bit. I didn't flinch or move away, so he moved his hand up.

"Do you wanna go someplace?" he said.

"Well, I'm goin to my friend Carla Cupcake's house."

"I can pick you up later on. When you comin back?"

"Yeah, it's a possibility. What's your name?"

He said his name was Nickie and he would pick me up in three hours. Then about six o'clock I left Carla's house and there he was waiting right where he dropped me off. I ran right over to the car.

He says, "Do you wanna have something to eat?"

"Okay, sure."

"What do you want?"

"Chinese food! I love Chinese food!"

We went to *Mark's Chinese Restaurant*. We had dinner, and on the way back he gave me a grab or two.

I don't know, I don't really feel comfortable, I'm not really sure if I wanna do this, so I said. "Actually, I used to fool around but I stopped cause I'm tryin to keep clear of it and do the right thing and change myself ... "

Which was all bullshit. I just wasn't sure if I wanted to do it or not. I didn't find him extremely attractive but I didn't find him repulsive. There was just something about him that wasn't sexual for me.

"All right, I can respect that," and he dropped me off and said, "I got some painting to do at my house. Would you like to come over and make some money?"

"Sure! I'm not goin to school now."

I had just stopped school and I was signed up for barber's school. I think I had a few weeks before the classes started. "Yeah, I could definitely paint. I have a friend of mine, could I bring him with me?"

"Sure," he said.

Nickie was probably 35 and I was fifteen. He was an older man. Meanwhile, Junior was my boyfriend and I was madly in love with him. Junior was a year younger than me, and he was straight, basically, but he fooled around with me only, just because he enjoyed fooling around. Actually, he had a girlfriend at the time, but I kind of made things happen and we ended up staying together for three or four years.

Nickie picked Junior and me up the following day after Junior got out of school. Junior was goin to New Dorp High School at the time. We went over and we started painting for him. After we painted Nickie took us out to dinner at *Mark's Chinese Restaurant* again. We painted for about three weeks. He had a three story house where he lived with his mother and father and his two younger brothers. One brother, Mario, was the same age as me.

Nickie would take us into Manhattan, drivin around. Then we would drop Junior off and he would try to fool around with me and sometimes I would and sometimes I wouldn't. He finally got the picture that Junior and I were foolin around together. He became like a sugar daddy and he would buy me clothes. He would say to me, do you wanna go shoppin, over at Korvette's.

"Yeah, I need pants, I need shoes." If I made fifty dollars I would buy fifty dollars worth of clothes, and then Nickie would say, no no, put your money away. And he would put his money up and I would say, *Oh, thank you, that's very nice of you.* It would happen maybe three or four times a week. I would have money left over, so the next day I wanted to go and pick up records, and I'd go and Nickie would say, no no, put your money away. And the day after that I'd say, well, bein that you didn't take money for the clothes and you didn't take money for the records, I have to go buy a jacket! So we would go for a jacket and Nickie would take his money out.

"You know, you really don't hafta do this. I have my own money, you're payin me."

"No, it's all right."

He was tryin to play the man and while he was tryin to play the man, I was playin him. It wasn't a nice thing to do, but I didn't come from much, my parents didn't have enough money and that's the way it was.

I wanted to plan a sweet sixteen birthday party for myself. I had a straight party and I called it quits at about eleven o'clock and at midnight my gay friends came over, probably about fifteen of us, and it was quite gay. My ex-girlfriend Marie seen the lights on and she came downstairs. She spoke to my niece, Murphy.

Marie said, "Murphy, what the hell's goin on here?"

"Didn't you figure it out?"

"There are a lot of strange people goin on here. It seems everybody is gay."

Murphy said, "Everybody *is* gay, including Fred."

"Oh," she said. "I can deal with that."

"Good, cause that's what the deal is. He really is gay."

"But he's been with me, together for a good year or so."

"And yeah, he's also been with Junior for over a year. And Nickie is hosting the party, he's kinda his sugar daddy."

Marie, you're sixteen years old now, it's time to figure out what life is all about.

By the time I was seventeen my father caught on and that's when he threw me out. Nickie got me a room in St. George. He said, "I would get an apartment, but I can't move out of the house because that's just not the way it's done. When you're Italian and you're a man, you live at home until you get married."

We used to go to a place called the Firehouse in Stapleton, that was opened by my friend Phil, who was gay. We used to go in there even though I was only seventeen. The night that my father threw me out we went to the Firehouse and this guy comes walkin in, Jimmy Jett, that I knew from high school. Jimmy and I used to fool around, so Jimmy said, "Why don't you come back later on?"

"Yeah, maybe I will."

Nickie dropped me off in St. George at my room, and I walked back to Stapleton. I picked up Jimmy and we walked back to the room and we fooled around. The next day Nickie and I went back to the Firehouse, and someone there must have said something to Nickie about it.

Nickie said to me, "C'mon, let's go."

"Okay."

We got into the car and he had a really bad attitude. My friend Abe was in the front seat. I got in the back seat,

"What are you gettin in the back seat for?"

"I don't like your attitude. You're gettin really nasty and I don't wanna sit next to you."

We're drivin down the street and Nickie says,

"What's goin on with you and Jimmy Jett? I heard you were with him, that you went back to the bar after I left."

"Yeah. What's the problem?" I was a bitch.

"You left with Jimmy Jett."

"You know, you don't own me."

And with that, he turned around and he punched me in my face.

I started kickin him from the backseat. Now he couldn't drive while I'm kickin him. He turned around and he gave me a backhand in the mouth. I was still kickin him though and he ended up hittin a fire hydrant. The car was on the fire hydrant and the fire hydrant was spewing out and I'm still kickin him. He opened up the car door and he fell out. I pushed the seat up, I got out and I ran back to the Firehouse.

"Phil, Phillie," I says. "Hide me quick, Nickie's after me!"

Nickie had to stay with the car because he had to get the car off of the fire hydrant.

"What the hell happened?" Phil said. I had blood comin out of my mouth and everything.

The old men sitting at the bar said, "What's the matter with you? You're playin with fire! You're takin everything from this man and you're not givin him nothin in return. You know what he wants. He brings you and your boyfriend in here and buys you drinks, and then he takes the both of you out to dinner, then he drives the both of you home, so you can have sex. And he goes home alone to his parents' house with his dick in his hand."

"All right," Phil said. "Get in the backroom, get in the kitchen."

And that's where I hid. When Nickie rushed in and asked if I had come back, they said no, and he rushed back out again without buyin a drink or nothin. I sat in the cold box until the bar closed.

Phil ended up drivin me back to my mother's to sleep in the basement overnight until I could go into the city. My father wasn't home, he was workin. Nickie had already been there, too. He had gone into my bedroom because all my stuff was still there because my father had just kicked me out. My mother was there and said, "Nickie, what's goin on?"

Nickie took every stitch of clothes that I had out of the closets. He ripped the wallpaper off the wall, because he paid for the wallpaper, he took the records, he took everything that he ever gave me. He packed it into the car and he left.

13. NORMAN PERKINS

Norman and I were very close friends. He came from Delaware but he became somewhat of an embarrassment to his parents so he didn't want to stay with them. He moved in with me and my parents, and he stayed there even after I left.

When he finally got his own apartment it was like a traveling circus. Fifteen or twenty-five of us would pile into Norman's apartment to go out and we would all do our makeup there. So how long would it be before the whole neighborhood was up and roaring and screaming, get em out of here!? These freaks, they're comin home at four, five o'clock in the morning dressed like women, drunk and disorderly. We were seventeen, eighteen, nineteen years old, so what did they expect?

He lived on Curtis Place and we used to hang out at the Mayfair Bar. That was the only gay bar in St. George. It was a safe haven, so to speak.

That's where we met Peter Fowler. He was a little guy with big, round eyeglasses. When we met him, he was freshly tossed out of the seminary. They threw him out because he was too gay.

"But I'm not gay," he told them.

"Yes, you are!" they said and they threw him out, him and his valise and a jar of pennies. When we first saw him he was counting out pennies to pay for his drink at the Mayfair. So we took him in under our wing.

One night, the three of us were at the Mayfair and Norman said, "I gotta change my shirt, I don't like this shirt. It makes me look fat. I gotta go home and change this shirt."

"Norman, would you stop it? Sit here, nobody gives a shit that you look fat."

"No no. I gotta change my shirt. I gotta change my shirt."

So Peter says, "All right, Norman, we'll go, we'll change your shirt. We'll go back, we'll walk all the way back to Curtis Place to change your shirt."

It's a hell of a walk. In the rain!

So they take the umbrella and they walk all the way up. They changed the shirt, it stopped raining. They're walking back with the umbrella down, and some guy stops and starts makin fun of them. Norman was like "Leave us alone!" And the guy started gettin really nasty and threw a punch at Norman.

Now, Norman Perkins was a big burly guy - six foot two. He was Polish and built like a Pole. But he was going, "Oh no! No! Don't hit me! No no!"

... and Peter was a skinny, little thing and he was sayin, "You bastard! You get the fuck away from my friend." He took the umbrella and said, "You bastard! You you you hurt my friend!" And he beat the hell out of the guy with the umbrella. The cops came and they wanted to arrest Peter and Norman for beatin up this guy.

They get back to the Mayfair, and Norman starts in right away.

"You'll never guess what happened! You'll never guess what happened! I was struck, they tried to mug us! They tried to mug us!"

"They didn't try to mug you. They beat you up because you're a fag."

"No, they tried to mug us!"

If Peter wasn't there, the story would've been about rape. Norman would have sworn that "they" were trying to rape him.

One day Norman wanted me to relax his hair. Before I went to hairdressing school, we were always dying each other's hair and doing each other's eyebrows, typical teenage girl stuff.

"I'm tired of having this curly hair. It's too curly I want it long and flowing like everybody else. I wanna relax it."

So he went out and he bought a relaxant. On the box it said you have to base the root, you have to put the relaxer a quarter of an inch away from the scalp. I didn't know what base meant, so we just skipped that part. (Base means you have to apply Vaseline or something to protect the scalp.) Then you need to go a quarter of an inch from the scalp away and I thought it meant a quarter of an inch on the scalp. So I put the relaxer right on the scalp and I placed it a quarter of an inch on the shaft of the hair, exactly where it was not supposed to be. Then they said, wait fifteen minutes and then rub it all through to the ends of the hair. So we left it there for fifteen minutes which is a total disaster, and then I started combing it through.

He said, "It's burning!"

I said, "Do you want me to wash it off?"

"No no no. Oh my God, it burns so bad!"

And I'm combing it to the ends.

"Oh, it burns so bad!"

I said, "Norman, it's not straight! I'm lookin and it's not..."

"Leave it on! Leave it on!"

So now another fifteen or twenty minutes went by. You're only supposed to bring it through for like five minutes. At that point I shampooed it off, we couldn't get it off.

He said, "My head. It hurts. It burns!" His whole scalp was bright red.

He said, "I just have to lay down. I have a headache."

He laid down. When he woke up two, three hours later, he couldn't get his head off of the pillow case. It was stuck to the pillow case. His scalp oozed. He had severe chemical burns all over his head. He had to go to the doctor. The doctor had to put all this stuff on his head to try to get the pillow case off. He had blisters on his scalp for weeks oozing something. What did we know? We still didn't know what the hell we done wrong until months later when we talked to somebody. At that time you never put a relaxer on the scalp. Nowadays you have relaxers that you can put right on the scalp. I done them when I had the salon, we did seventy-five percent black hair in St. George so we learned how to do relaxers. It's a piece of cake once you know how to do it.

Years later, I said to Norman, "Do you want me to do a relaxer on you?"

"NO!"

"But I know how to do it now..."

"No! Never again! No! No!"

We worked together quite a bit. We were close friends, and we cross dressed all the time. He was very into glamor and that would be our hobby. I was seventeen, he was eighteen, we would paint ourselves, do whatever we could. Then later on in life when we had jobs, we would go to the balls together. When the clubs started opening up on Staten Island and I started workin, I said, come do shows with me and he was part of the review that we did all over. He was very good to work with, he was artsy and talented and he sewed. He would have great ideas for scenery and costumes.

He was fun to work with but he was schizophrenic also and he would go off on the other end. He would tell fabulous lies. Like he got bit by a tsetse fly in New Jersey. He had a boat and the boat ran aground on a sandbar and while he was on the sandbar he got bit by a tsetse fly so he had "global pneumonia" and encephalitis and he was unconscious. He was in a coma for six months. He told this story to many, many people. One time I had him to dinner and my next door neighbor at the time was a nurse. She laughed.

"Oh, Norman, you're so funny."

"What do mean, I'm funny?"

"You couldn't possibly have been unconscious for six months. There would be total brain damage. Well,... I see some...but..."

"What do you mean?"

"You would probably be paralyzed for the rest of your life, or you wouldn't have the use of your arms.... Six months of being totally in a coma?"

"Yes, I was in a coma for six months, with global pneumonia!"

"And you just came out of it?"

"Yes!"

"It just doesn't happen that way."

"Are you callin me a liar? I don't like...."

... and he would go on and on and get insulted and he would walk out when someone called him on his shit. So all of us would just roll our eyes and here comes another one.

He was working for Alan Brazil who had a club in South Beach called Club Brazil and we did shows there and Norman tended bar also. Norman comes in one night,

"Oh My God!"

Alan was on the day shift and Norman was taking over the night shift, so Alan was behind the bar. Alan looked over and said *oh no I'm not gonna ask him what's wrong.*

"I Can't Believe It!" and Norman banged his hands on the bar.

And Alan looked up and said *I'm not gonna say nothin.*

"I Can't Believe It Happened Again!"

....

"I Just Can't Believe It!"

And finally someone said, "What happened, Norman?"

"I Lost The Keys To The Vault In The Bank And All The Family Jewels Are In There! My Mother Is Gonna Kill Me! They're Gonna Think I'm Crazy At The Bank!"

"The keys to the vault?"

"Yes! And All The Family Jewels Are There! My Mother Trusted Me To Hold Onto The Keys. And Now I Lost Them Again. I Have To Go All The Way To Delaware And I Have To Do This That And The Other Thing..."

I met the family once, when I borrowed my father's car to drive him to Delaware to get some clothes. They lived in a little cold water flat. They were the sweetest little Polish couple, as poor as church mice.

Yes, the keys to the vault.

When I went to hairdressing school he was working at Goldsmith Bros. and he wanted to sue them because he cut his finger on a piece of glass in one of their showcases. It was a scratch, a teensy weensy nothing and he called in work the next day.

"I can't come in. I think it's infected I have to go see my family doctor."

They were like, all right, call in.

He called back the next day and he said, "No, my doctor says that I need complete bed rest and its very, very serious."

"Listen, if you're not gonna come, we're gonna have to fire you. It's not a very hard job to do and we need somebody here to do it. If you can't do it, somebody else can."

"I can't believe it! I'm gonna sue you people!"

Of course, it never went nowhere, but once again, he was out of work. I said, Norman why don't you go to hairdressing school? So he went to hairdressing school and he got his license and I hired him because I had the salon then. But it was the same thing. You got him on a good day, he was fabulous, there was nobody better. He was creative, he was funny. But when you got him on his bad day, oh my

God, he may as well just walk in and say, *fuck all of you, I ain't stayin,* because that's what it would come down to.

He wouldn't talk to people, if he did it was somethin nasty.

"Norman, your next customer is here."

"Yeah? Well, so what? I'm still workin on this one, and I'm not gonna push her aside for the other one."

"There was no need to say that, you know."

"Well, what am I supposed to say?"

"Thank you... Okay... I'll be with her as soon as I can..."

"Well, you're sayin it to me like I have to jump right on it!"

"I just said your next customer is in, to let you know. I said the same thing to you yesterday and you were fine with it."

"Well, if that's the way you wanna be, I'll just leave."

And he would throw his brush down and walk out. The next day he'd call and say, "I'm really sorry, I don't know what came over me."

"The two customers you had there are never comin back again."

There was no Zoloft then.

He was a gay cross dressing, poor Howard Hughes, with overtones of Ethel Merman. If he had money, he would've hired the Mormons to take care of him, and not cut his fingernails. If he had money...but he didn't have money. The last thing I heard, he was taking care of old women. Somehow he found a lot of old women, maybe one told the other. If you were an old woman and you had nobody to take care of you and you had money, Norman would come and he would cook food for you or at least order food for you, tidy up your house a little bit, and drive you to the post office or the hairdresser, basically your companion. I guess his whole gig was that he figured that sooner or later one of them was gonna die and leave him all the money. But it was more like Baby Jane. Would you leave Baby Jane your money?

"Blanche! Eat the bird! Blanche!"

14. NICKIE THROUGH THE YEARS

When I was twenty-one, I worked at Joseph's. It was a truck stop, a diner during the day but at night they had no business, so they contacted me and said, could you run it as a gay bar.

"Get a couple of friends of yours to tend bar, work the door, whatever you have to do. Fags don't cause no trouble, so we'll leave you alone, we don't want nothin to do with it. Just make the money, and leave the money in the register and that's it."

So I got a hold of Norman Perkins and Dotty Kenny, and the three of us ran the bar. It was fun. I think we did it for about six months, that's the run of a gay bar on Staten Island. A year tops. Then it sort of goes the way of the cuckoo, one way or another.

All of our friends came. It was a big crowd. We would get about a hundred people per night that would come in every weekend. Then late at night, after the bar closed up, somebody would run an after hours party. So everybody would pile over to Audrey's house or somewhere and we would party until the sun came up.

At this time, I hadn't seen Nickie for two years. I'm behind the bar one night and in walks Nickie. *Oh my God, he's gonna kill me.* He sits down at the bar. He's with this other guy, who's about my age, nineteen, very serious lookin, very straight lookin kid.

This is it. He's gonna have me murdered or somethin. He musta found out I'm workin here. He's gonna kill me.

He says, "How ya doin?"

"I'm doin fine, Nickie. How are you?"

"I'm doin good. This is Dick Sweet, this is Freddie."

"Yeah, I heard a lot about you, Freddie."

"Did ya? Whataya have to drink?"

I gave them their drinks, two or three drinks. Later I asked Norman, who was also tending bar, "Watch the bar for me. I have to go to the bathroom."

I'm by the urinal. The door opens up and I turn around and look, and it's Dick Sweet.

Oh my God, he's gonna beat me up right here in the bathroom.

He turns off the bathroom light, walks over to me in the dark and kisses me.

"What the fuck is this all about? Nickie is gonna kill the both of us!"

"No, no, it's cool."

"Cool? Are you out of your mind? I know this man, he's gonna kill the both of us! You're with him. That's what you're doin with him, you're fuckin around with him."

"Yeah, but I like you."

"No, no, he's gonna kill the both of us. This man has a background. He's connected. The whole family is connected. You just can't do things like this."

I ran out of the bathroom and went back to the bar. Now I'm a nervous wreck, I'm shakin, I'm droppin things, I'm wide eyed, I'm like what the fuck is goin on? ... and they're stayin, it's two o'clock in the morning, it's three o'clock. I call last call. Nickie is still sittin there with Dick. Now it's Norman, Dotty Kenny, me, Nickie and Dick Sweet.

Nickie says to me, "Do you need a ride home?"

"No, I'm gonna call a cab."

"No, I'll give you a ride home."

"What's this all about?"

"Dick likes you."

"And you're okay with that?"

"Yeah, I'm okay with that."

"I don't understand."

"Don't worry about it."

"All right."

I got into the car.

Nickie says, "You want company?"

"What are you talkin about?"

"I gotta go home, you know I can't stay out. So I'll leave Dick with you and I'll pick him up tomorrow in the afternoon when I'm on my way to work."

"You're gonna leave Dick with me? You know somethin is goin to happen."

"Of course I know something is goin to happen."

Dick and I made love until eleven a.m. It was just phenomenal. I was in love with Dick and Dick was infatuated with me. Nickie picked the Sweet one up that afternoon and everything was cool. This was what happened for the next couple of months. Nickie would come back and forth and drop him off and pick him up.

Then Dick showed up one day and said, "C'mon, I want you to go to Florida with me."

"I can't go to Florida. Where's Nickie?"

"I'm leavin him."

"He's payin for your apartment in Manhattan on Canal Street. And you're just gonna up and walk out? He doesn't know about this?"

"No, he doesn't know about this. C'mon, I want you with me."

"No, no, Dick. Now you're pushin the limit. Besides the fact that I'm still seein Junior. I still like Junior, I'm not ready to make a decision like that... Dick, you're like a bad boy."

Dick was a hustler, havin sex for money. He was doin some crazy shit in Manhattan. I wasn't into anything like that.

"I don't wanna be a part of that. Nickie is gonna end up killin ya. I'm tellin ya. Nickie is gonna end up beatin the shit out of ya."

"I'm gonna go. If you don't wanna go, I'm gonna go myself."
"Then go yourself."
And he did, he left.

Nickie followed him down about a month later and smacked him around quite a bit and brought him back to Manhattan. Dick was, I'm sorry,... I won't do it again.... It was uncool.

They ended up breakin up again, and Dick Sweet went his own way.

Nickie and I became very good friends after that. I moved in with my new boyfriend Frankie. Nickie used to come to dinner all the time, he saw me through my relationships, after Frankie it was Booboo, then Leon. When I bought the house I consulted with Nickie. There was no sex between us, it was just a very good friendship.

Now I was twenty-one and I got the salon in New Dorp, where Nickie lived, and his family came to me to get their hair done. His sister came in, his brothers all came in for haircuts, his mother and father came in. Nickie would come in and hang out every day before work, hang out for an hour or two, have lunch with me. He knew everybody there. We were like family, his family was like my family. I used to spend Christmas over there, holidays.

One day his sister was at the salon and we were talkin about my relationship with Leon and his sister says to me, "It's a shame that Nickie doesn't have anybody."

"What are you talkin about?"

"Nickie, he's had so many boyfriends, but nothin seems to last."

...

"You know about Nickie?"

"The whole family knows about Nickie, since he was in high school."

"Get outta here! Nobody ever says nothin to him?"

"Nah, it's not the right thing to do, if he wants to keep it a secret."

"You know, he thinks that nobody knows about him. How many opportunities he coulda had. He had an apartment in Manhattan with Dick Sweet."

She said, "Oh yeah, I remember Dick. He was a nice boy. He used to work with Nickie."

"Yeah. They were lovers," I said.

"Oh."

Nickie had a truck route and Dick Sweet would help him now and then on the truck as a helper. Dick had the apartment in Manhattan and Nickie used to stay there until three o'clock in the mornin and then drive home and wake up in the mornin and go to work and after work go to Dick's house, go to the movies, go out until three o'clock in the morning and go home again... But he would never sleep out, because the family would get suspicious.

"But we all knew about him since high school!"

"Oh my God, that's terrible! You need to talk."

"No, it's not the right thing to do."

Then his younger brother Mario started comin in for haircuts. Mario was definitely beyond a doubt gay. He went to school with my friend Abe, who told me he was gay. So I told Mario, "You know, Abe told me about you."

"Oh, he's got a big mouth."

"Yeah, but it's cool."

"Yeah, I know you and Nickie were foolin around."

"Yeah, so you're gay, right?"

"Yeah, totally gay, absolutely."

"So why don't you talk to Nickie."

"No, my brother doesn't want to talk about shit like that. He's very closed mouth, ... old school."

I said, "That's ridiculous."

So it was known that they knew about each other. I told Nickie, I told Mario, Nickie knew about Mario, Mario knew about Nickie. Nickie would bring home guys that were twenty years younger than him because he had a thing for young guys. He would introduce them, this is my friend from work, and Mario and the rest of the family knew what was goin on. Then he would drop them off at my house, they would sleep over in the guest room. Then he would pick them up in the morning. It was Nickie leading a double life all the time. It was really a shame.

He was the generation before me and that was the generation where you just didn't come out. He came from that old school and it was a sad thing because they knew all the time, but in that generation you just didn't tell your kid that you know. You didn't make waves, even though you knew. The poor guy was forty and fifty and sixty years old and he was still playin games for his parents, for the family, meanwhile the whole family knew. His own brother knew and they never talked to each other about boyfriends or whatever. The two of them, Nickie and Mario, would even come to parties that I had, that were totally, absolutely gay. Nickie would be there with his boyfriend. They wouldn't be huggin and kissin or dancin. Mario would be there, he didn't have a boyfriend at this time. They were comfortable with it, but words were never said, looks were never exchanged, there was never anything good, bad or indifferent said about their relationships.

I think it could have been a whole lot happier, it would have been really nice. His father, for instance, used to joke around with me all the time, pinch me on the cheek, and say things, "Aren't you the sweetie! Oh, if I didn't marry my wife, Tina, you woulda been in trouble!" Tina used to laugh and he used to laugh. In front of his wife he used to say stuff like this. It was all a joke, but it was very obvious that his father knew exactly where I was comin from. He'd say, "Are you and Leon comin over for dinner, New Year's Day?"

We were family, we did everythin together. Nickie was in the coven with me, he was also a pagan priest. He was with me when Leon passed away. It was him that took me to the funeral, that comforted me and saw me through. He was probably one of my best friends and an important role model, somebody that taught me how to be what people expected me to be, even to the point of danger. He used to take me to the social club that John Gotti used to run. On a Saturday night we would go to Manhattan and we would go to the social club first because he had to see a few people.

"Look, when you go in there, you keep your hands in your pockets. You don't talk, you just nod. If someone asks you if you want a drink, you say, no thank you, that's all, or just shake your head no, or nod your head yes. Do as less talkin as you possibly can, and don't take your hands out of your pockets, unless you have a drink in your hands, because you start wavin your hands around and you start gettin flamboyant and everything and everybody's gonna know everything about you and they're gonna figure it out about me."

There were a lot of things that I can't even talk about, like the time when there was a lot of counterfeit money goin around ... that was a funny time, to say the least. Everybody was mob related and you had to be careful. His uncles certainly were. His mother and father would tell me stories about the uncles. You would never take a favor from any of them, because if you take a favor, they expect a favor. If somebody offers you something, you say no thank you ... *that's very generous of you, but no thank you, I'd rather not.* You don't say yes to any of that stuff. If you never take nothin, then they can never ask you for nothin. But if you start takin things, sooner or later they're gonna ask you for a favor, a service or somethin and you'll be sorry.

15. LUCILLE

Lucille was one of the lights in my life who helped me see my way to where I am today. Her father had a beauty salon supply store in Asbury Park, New Jersey, DiRoma Supply Store. She took over when her father passed away and she got the exclusive contract to open salons in Grant's Department Store, a chain of stores like Kmart.

She took a loan for the furniture. She furnished and supplied the stores and Grant's took a percentage of what they pulled in monthly and gave her the rest. Grant's would come around six times a day and empty out the register. At the end of the month they would send her a check from each Grant's Department store. She had hairdressers and managers and they all got a percentage of what they made. She had about 50 salons in Grant's Department Stores all over New York, New Jersey and Pennsylvania.

It was a pretty good deal for her. She was intelligent and she had a wonderful poker face that she would put on. She came from an Italian background, had a sweetheart of a mother, a little old Italian lady. The mother loved to cook, she hardly had schooling but she brought up three, four children: earthy, plain, loving. Then when you met Lucille, you said, oh my God, this has to be big college material, she had to have a master's in business or something. She presented herself with savoir faire, she commanded respect and attention. She would walk in and people were just like, Ooh, Lucille's here. If you had something you really needed to know, "Ask Lucille, she'll know."

She had the salons about four or five years. She was in the supply house, doing all the bills and ordering and her sister Roseanne was in charge of all the bookwork, accounting, controlling things. The third sister, Joan, was in charge of supplies, she packed supplies and sent them out. Then at a certain point, Lucille met a guy and married him, and from then on, the three sisters ran things in the background and Lucille's husband, Syd, went around to all 50 salons, to check up on things, hire and fire people.

Syd was gone most of the time and she was pregnant. She said, *something's wrong with this picture. I have a funny feeling and I'm gonna hire a detective to watch Syd.* She found out that Syd was stealing from the salons and that he was fooling around with a lot of the female managers. He would buy shears at twenty dollars a pair and sell them to the people that worked there at a hundred and fifty dollars a pair. And here she was working like a maniac, now with a set of twins on her hip in the supply house.

He came home one evening in his five hundred dollar suit from one of his long trips, two weeks or whatever it was. He found his suitcases all on the front steps. He banged on the door and said, "What's this?"

"Well, you'd better read the note that's there."

"What the hell are you talkin about? What is this?"

"Go. Go. You need to get out of here. You'll be served with papers. This is over. I'm not playin games here."

That's exactly when I met Lucille. My boyfriend Booboo was working in Grant's Department Store and he told Lucille about me. All the salons were fairly low budget and she had all these people that worked for her that were just out of school. She needed to give them the confidence and the education to be able to keep up with the times. I was working in a small salon on Staten Island and doing very well, so she asked me if I wanted to travel around to a couple of the different salons and teach cutting and coloring.

"Lucille, I don't know if I can do it."

"Oh, you can do it."

We went around and I just picked up on how she presented herself to people and I mimicked that.

A couple of months after that she wanted me to go someplace on a Saturday.

"Lucille, there is no way they're gonna let me go on a Saturday. They need me in the salon on Saturdays."

"How about if I open up a salon for you?"

I knew a salon close by that I had worked in that was closed down for a year, I knew where the pipes were for the plumbing and I knew the electric was all in. That's the biggest problem. The rest is a piece of cake.

"So let's do it," she said.

She pulled together the furniture from one of the salons, I did the wallpaper and the painting. We hired people and we were up and running in three weeks. I left the place I was at and I took my following, a small following, not nearly enough for a salon. She said, "That's fine, it's a base for you, you can do photos from here. It doesn't have to be makin money for me. So long as it pays you a salary and you can come and go as I want you to, that's all that really matters."

Terrific!

She paid double and triple on her monthly installments to get them paid off quicker. Then one day she said, "You know what, now that I'm just about ready to make my last payment on the furniture. I think I'm gonna go on vacation for the first time."

She went to Puerto Rico. Two or three days into the trip she went out to get coffee and the New York papers. She sat down someplace and had a cigarette. She opened up the papers and it said, *Grant's Department Stores bankrupt. Closes their doors after so many years in business!*

She was, Oh my God, what happened to all my salons? She ran to the phone and called the main office. She couldn't get through, it was busy constantly.

Booboo calls me and says, "They just came in and said we're bankrupt! They said, you've got an hour and a half to get out of here. You've got to clear out, because we're closin the doors. So take whatever you can carry, because once we close the doors, nothing can be gotten. It's lost! What should we do?"

"Put everything in shopping carts and bring it over here ... and the first thing you put in is the register."

So he put the register in and the girls that worked there put rollers, dryers everything in shopping carts and started running a block and a half down to my salon. The people that were in the dryers at Grant's had to go. So here are all the customers coming down Hylan Boulevard with shopping carts, a woman with rollers in her hair, with permanent wave rods in her hair. "Quick, quick! You gotta rinse her down! She's got to be neutralized!"

It was a fiasco.

All the people that worked in Grant's came over. They brought all of their clients into my salon.

Lucille tried to get a plane back that day, but she couldn't get a flight and she had to wait until the next day. She said, "There was nothin I could do. I ordered up a couple of piña coladas and went to sleep until the next morning." She went to Jersey and Oh my God, what are we gonna do?

She was told that because she was renting a space in Grant's, the store was not entitled to her furniture. She had three weeks to get it all out, but after that the fixtures would be sold.

"How can I get fifty salons in three weeks?"

So I said, "The only thing you can do is call all the managers, give them a week's pay or whatever it takes and tell them to get a hold of a local moving business and put all the furniture in a moving van and send it to Asbury Park.

"Where am I going to put it?"

"Asbury Park! You have all these big old empty buildings. It's like a ghost town anyway, you're bound to be able to rent one of the buildings."

So she rented a building. She called me up when they started to come, "I don't know what the heck to do!"

So I ran down to Asbury Park. We got people on the boardwalk, winos. "C'mon, you can work for ten dollars an hour."

"Oh, we'll do it gladly."

"And if you get somebody for us, we'll give you ten dollars to get somebody in."

"Okay, we'll do it!"

So we emptied out all the trucks.

A couple of weeks after that she calls me and says, "How would you like to own the salon?"

I said, "Lucille, there's no way in the world. I could never...I couldn't possibly...I don't have the intelligence, I don't know how to do the bookwork, the taxes, the payroll."

She says, "How are you fixed for money?"

"I'm not! I just bought that house! I don't have the money. It's ridiculous. I couldn't possibly do it."

"Fred, you can do it. Drive down to Asbury Park."

"Okay, I'll drive down but I don't think I can do it."

I got into the office. There she was with her two lawyers. They had it all signed up. "How much can you afford?"

I said, "I can't afford it! I really can't do it!"

She gave me the salon for five thousand dollars, two thousand dollars, a ridiculous amount of money. She gave it to me.

"Lucille, I can't do the paperwork."

"I'll come down every Friday. You'll do my hair, I'll do the paperwork, I'll teach you how."

I said, "All right, I can't say no to that."

She set me up. She set me up completely.

The week after that, I get a phone call from the next shopping center over. There was another budget salon, Sam's and a girl that I grew up with, Happy, worked there. She said, "Sam's is closin down, he's goin bankrupt. I got four girls that are workin with me. Can we come over there and work?"

I said, "Come on over!"

So now I had all these operators. It was phenomenal. We were open seven days a week until nine o'clock every night. It was a fantastic business. Lucille came every week and she taught me how to do the bookwork. But it was her confidence in me, it was her willingness to sell me the salon for such a ridiculous amount of money. If it wasn't for her, I couldn't possibly have made it in the world. Probably the brightest light in my business career was Lucille. I can't thank her enough. I used to try to thank her and she would poo poo it. "Stop. Stop. Don't be ridiculous."

"Lucille, if it wasn't for you..."

"Stop. Stop."

16. ARRIVAL IN PUERTO RICO

The first person to put makeup on me was Fernando, whose stage name was Gypsy. Gypsy was a stripper and she did impersonations of Diana Ross and Shirley Bassey. Fernando was also a fantastic dressmaker. He used to make a lot of my costumes for me. When Fernando was Fernando, he was all boy. He came from Puerto Rico and he had a dress salon there. We met in St. George in the Mayfair when I was about eighteen. Fernando, myself, Norman Perkins and Peter all met together the same week and we became fast friends for a long time.

Fernando had an apartment near the Mayfair with an older man, his lover. He was having a Halloween party and he was gonna dress and perform. He wanted everyone else to dress too. I said, "I don't think so, I can't do my makeup that well, I only put lipstick on."

He says, "Come up to the apartment, let me do some makeup on ya."

He was the first one to put eyeliner on me. I looked in the mirror and went, "This is it! I love it!" The eyeliner was something that put me right over the top.

He says, "There is always something that when you put it on, that's when you become your female persona, be it lipstick ... a wig ... "

Mine was eyeliner, as soon as that eyeliner went on, I was like "Oh, my goodness, Fernando this is fabulous! I gotta learn how to do this!"

I went home and learned how to do my eyeliner the way that Fernando did it.

... and I went to the party. My mom made me a gown.

When I was 21, Frankie, me and Carlos went to Puerto Rico. Fernando was working at a club there as a bartender and he did shows every Saturday and Sunday. When we got there Fernando said, come on, do the backup for the Supremes. I'm doin Diana Ross, and you can do the backup, do the Supremes. He talked us into it, we did the whole thing in blackface, coco colored makeup. Fernando made us gowns and it was fabulous.

The club was Juni's in old San Juan. Juni was a lesbian and her girlfriend was with her, it was one big happy family. Everybody that worked in the bar were all friends, the waiters and the bartenders and Connie Kilowatt, the electrician, and Suzy the maid who would open up the bar in the morning. She was a cross dresser and extremely slow. We would go to the beach together in the afternoon, with four to six to eight blankets and we'd all be sittin there with sandwiches and beer and soda carrying on all day long, listening to music. Then in the late afternoon we would run around and give everybody on the beach fliers, "Come to Juni's!"

Then long about five o'clock we would run back to Juni's and we'd rehearse for a while, then we would do our hair and do our makeup and we'd go out on the balcony. Juni had a three story building. The second story was where the bar was and there was a big balcony right off the stage. We would open up the doors for the breeze to come in during the day and we would go out there and cool off. We were rehearsing with hair and makeup on and we would have shorts and no shirts on because it was so hot. We would be standin on the balcony and the people walking back and forth would see four drag queens with no tits. They would be waving to us and screamin. Across the street was a daytime bar that Bobby Ray used to run. He was also a performer. It was four shutters that would open up and behind them was one bar fifteen, twenty-five feet long, one bar straight across. The stools were on the sidewalk. People would sit on the sidewalk and have drinks. He would scream up, oh, girls how you doin? What time is the show. Oh Bobby, how are you. It was insanity on the streets of San Juan.

The third floor, the roof, really, was where the dressing room was. After we were done dressing before the performance, we would go over to the edge of the roof and there were three planks going across from that building to the next building. We would take off our heels and walk across to the next building, to Arturo's gay guesthouse. He had a rooftop bar and we would sit there and have a drink before the show. Then we would walk back across the planks and downstairs to do our show.

We performed Friday, Saturday and Sunday for two weeks, and as Fernando told everybody, the last night we were gonna do our farewell performance at midnight. We did, "Ain't no mountain high enough." They were throwin flowers at us and they were bringin stuffed animals up on the stage. We finished the number and there was a standing ovation and people cryin, huggin us. You'd think we were really the Supremes the way they were carryin on.

I got on the plane and I cried. I don't wanna go home, I love this place, I love these people. It's one of the few places that I can go back to and walk around the same streets I walked around. I can sit on the same corner that I sat on in the same exact place. I can touch the same stone that I touched then. All those things mean a lot to me. I like to go to the places that Leon and I went to, that Fernando took us to, like the steps that the Flying Nun runs down in the opening and closing as the credits come on.

Going back to Puerto Rico almost every year, I feel that Puerto Rico is my home. When I die I would love to die in Puerto Rico. As soon as I get off the plane I can smell that special air. When I get to the beach I can smell that special seaweed. Even if I go alone, I walk on those streets and I feel like I belong there.

Years later Fernando was living in Philadelphia. He worked in a bar called the Pigpen. We used to drive down there three or four times a year, Nickie and Frankie and Leon and myself. We would sleep on his living room floor.

Then we were busy and I wasn't goin over there so much anymore. I hadn't talked to him in over a year. One afternoon Leon and I went down because Leon had a photo shoot with a dressmaker named Mister Steele. Leon was Mister Steele's pinup boy. Steele designed for performers like the Pointer Sisters. He did leather and lace. Whenever he did a garment and he wanted to have it for a photo presentation he was doing, he would always have Leon dressed in almost nothing in the photo. There would be a woman in this fabulous leather and lace gown and Leon would be sitting on the floor with his legs crossed so you couldn't see that he was wearing anything, a thong. Mister Steele used Leon in his photos as his logo or something. I think he just wanted Leon, but I always went along with Leon, so he never got the chance.

We used to do the makeup for the girls and after doin the hair, Leon would stand in. I said, *let me call Fernando*. It was later in the day, so I called up the bar.

"Can I speak to Fernando?"

"Oh I have some very sad news for you, Fernando passed away last week."

"Oh my God, of what?"

"Of AIDS."

"I didn't even know."

"It was very, very quick."

I was completely devastated. I hung up the phone and said, "I need to go out for a walk."

"What's the matter?" Leon said.

"I'll tell you later."

I didn't want to ruin the photo shoot for him. I walked around for an hour or two.

That was the height of the plague. Fernando was a year before Leon, then it was Robin only a few months before Leon and Carlos two or three months after Leon. It was a devastating time. People say you forget in time. You don't forget a thing. As a matter of fact, I think you remember more and you add to memories. Those wonderful good times, you enhance and the bad times you muffle. Your memories ripen and they become so very sweet.

17. ANTONIA AND THE BOYS FROM BOYSBARN

Right after I met Leon and he started working in the salon in New Dorp, we had a client named Mona. Mona's mother was an Alsatian gypsy and pagan and very "old world" but Mona was totally uninterested. She was a typical girl of the fifties, all involved with modern stuff, all TV dinners and canned ravioli. One day Mona brought in her daughter Antonia, who was just back from Canada. Antonia was an old soul like her grandmother. Though the grandmother never outwardly talked about it, there were traditions and ceremonies that she would bring Antonia through, because Antonia was interested at a very early age. At the age of nine she was reading a book a week and she was cooking with her grandmother, learning about herbs. They would always light a candle for the new moon and a candle for the full moon.

She got interested in paganism. She moved to Canada and she met William and Tamara, who had started the Wiccan Church of Canada. She got totally involved and helped them set up the church. She came back from Toronto because she had a baby there and she wanted to raise the baby on her own. She didn't want to marry the father; he was a biker, a very nice guy named Bear, a big six foot three bear of a man, a sweetheart - but she just didn't want to be married to him.

We got together every Friday night. At one point she said, "My friend Rebekka runs a coven in Brooklyn. She's having Hallowmass circle, would you like to come?"

Leon and I said definitely!

When we got to Rebekka's house there were maybe twenty-four people there. We went into circle with them. After circle, Antonia said, "I'm gonna go out to the backyard to have a cigarette."

We went out with her and she said, "How did you like it?"

"Antonia, it feels like we're home."

After the ceremony was over we had a big feast. For two hours we ate and talked and sang and played music. Rebekka was a wonderful singer and a flute player and everybody involved in this coven was very musical.

Once a week on Saturday night after the shop closed we would do lessons. Antonia would give us different books to read and she would talk about the books. Carlos started coming every week, Nickie started coming for lessons also and Leon and me made four. We found a great joy in paganism.

We continued going to Rebekka's coven in Brooklyn. Antonia would call her and Rebekka would say, "Are you bringing the boys?"

"Of course!" Antonia said, "All four of them!"

"Oh, Antonia's bringing all the boys from Boysbarn!" Rebekka would announce. It was like the pagan, uncivilized version of Boystown. Antonia and the boys from Boysbarn is what they started calling us, and soon so did everyone else. And that's the origin of the name Boysbarn for the twenty-two room house on Fingerboard Road.

About two months into this we asked Antonia, "What is the next step? Where do we go from here?"

"Actually," she said, "To be pagan, the goal is to be your own priest or priestess. You should not be relying on others. Everyone should be dedicated as a priest or a priestess just to be able to take care of themselves and others. The preparation is usually about a year or a year and a half."

I said, "Why is it so long?"

"There are certain questions that people have to answer."

She asked the first question, and all of us answered it, then she asked the second, the third and the fourth. Some people take two or three years to answer these questions. We answered them in the time that it took us to park the car at an Indian restaurant and walk two blocks to the entrance.

Antonia: "That's absolutely amazing. You all answered it exactly the way they're supposed to be answered!"

(It's a process of elimination and when you finally eliminate all the things that are obvious, then you find the thing that is super-obvious, and that's the answer.)

We went over it for a couple more weeks and we took our initiation and our dedications and we started our elemental pacts with Earth, Air, Fire and Water and with the quarters, Summer, Winter, Spring and Fall. The first year of the pact you introduce yourself to the Air in the springtime. You only do four pacts a year and it takes you four years to finish all the sixteen pacts.

In the second year, the particular element and quarter introduces itself to you and in the third year you make an agreement and in the fourth year, you come together as bonded friends. Every quarter we would go out and do these pacts. Probably one of the most beautiful times of my life were those four years doing pacts. We would go away to the Poconos, go into the woods, go into the mountains. It brought us an amazing amount of spirituality that carried me through many things, made me appreciate myself, other people, things around me, gave me far more tolerance and grounded me. It brought us together as a coven that was very tight and very strong.

18. ALAN BRAZIL AND THE OLD JACK O' CLUBS

During the time that I worked at Joseph's, the truck stop, Alan came in one night with a friend of his. The friend ordered a drink.

I said, "I'm gonna have to see proof, you look very young!"

Somebody at the bar said, "Alan!"

He turned around and said, "Oh, Mr. So-and-so."

"What are you doin in here?" the man said. "He's in my class in high school!"

"Oh my God, I can't serve you," I said.

"You're not servin him!"

"Oh come on, Mr. So-and-so. Give us a break!"

"You can stay, you can drink soda, but I can't serve you liquor. Cops know it's a gay bar. They're gonna come in here and bust balls, they're gonna see somebody underage drinkin, I'm not gonna get in trouble for this, no way."

And his teacher also said, "I'm not gonna allow this. No. not happenin."

That's how I met Alan Brazil.

Alan Brazil went to Vietnam when he got old enough and he came back and he worked at Cheecho's, another bar in South Beach.

The club was in back of a funeral home. It first opened many years ago as a speakeasy, a big old house with a speakeasy in the basement. Then it was dormant for years, and then a Mafia man opened it up for his girlfriend to run, he put a piano bar in there, something to keep her busy. She was the cumara (in this case, the girlfriend) and he wasn't with her twenty-four seven, he had a wife and children. She was the hostess. Then it was closed for a long time, then my parent's friend, Nathan Stoutmeyer was going to open it with his friend Jack, and they called it the Jack of Clubs.

They asked my father to bartend. He was there for five or six years and then the bar got closed down because there was a murder, somebody got shot by the cigarette machine at the front door. It was always mob related. It stayed closed for a while, then it opened up as another mob bar. He opened it up as a gay bar called Cheecho's. He wasn't gay but he and his sons ran the place and his wife Maria would come in and cook.

Alan would tell me stories about Cheecho's. There'd be a party goin on. Cheecho's wife would be cookin sausage and peppers, whatever, the typical layout for a buffet. Alan would be in the kitchen and Maria would say, "Gimme the pan over there. Yeah, the one that's got all the black on the side. I would never use this at home for my family, but it's good enough for *them*."

Alan would look at her like, *Oh, my God!*

It's good enough for them. The fags are all right with this.

He would be there in the day tending bar. They would call him up and say, "Someone's comin down. We have a meeting down there, so be in at five o'clock because I have six people comin down."

Alan would clean up the bar nicey, nicey and the limousines would pull up. The wise guys would get out and come in with their suits and ties and sit down at the bar, talkin business. Then they would go in the back where they would talk real business. Alan would serve them drinks, and they'd say, Ah, buy everybody a round on me ... Ah, now you buy a round, ... now I buy everybody a round.

There was Nora, another bartender, a pistol packin dyke and a nasty bitch.

And there was a big shot named Ratz.

"Hey, Ratz, how ya doin?"

"I'm doin fine, Alan. How ya doin... Y'know, I gotta ask you a question, Alan. Nora, y'know Nora, and that's her girlfriend that tends bar here with her?"

"Yeah."

"I gotta ask you a question. Which one is the man? Who goes down on who?"

He didn't mean any harm, he was a nice old man but he had that rough edge.

They would spend four or five hundred dollars in the two hours they were there. That's the way to do things. You support other mob bars. They would leave and they would leave Alan a fifty dollar tip each, a hundred dollar tip if they were really big spenders. Alan would be like, this is more money in two hours than I made all month!

You have to show the respect and you have to show the clout you have, you have to show I'm the big man here.

We started doin drag shows there. It felt odd working there. I told my father, "Guess where I'm workin, doin shows?"

"Where you workin?"

"The old Jack o' Clubs."

"I heard somebody was gonna open a gay bar down there!"

"Did you really?"

"Yeah. Cheecho."

Later on, Alan bought Cheecho's and re-opened it as Brazil. He called it Brazil because he had gone there and he loved it so much. Then we did shows there all the time, and we would also meet down there to go to the city.

Three or four people would get there at seven o'clock, at eight o'clock there would be four or five more. Other people would come in and we would still be waitin for somebody that was too busy, couldn't decide what they were gonna wear, so they wouldn't show up until nine o'clock. So we were in there drinking from seven o'clock till nine o'clock. Then when the last person came, we would all run into the city to some big disco for two or three hours.

We'd be in the city and whoever got bored would say, "You know what, I'm goin back to Brazil. I'll meet you there later."

Then we would come back at three o'clock in the mornin, and spend an hour back there with Alan and our friends for the last hour that the bar was open, buy another two or three drinks and then go home.

People would call up and say, "Alan, who's there?"

Alan would say, "Oh, Norman's here and Freddie's here and Frankie's here, and Lana's here and her cousin Jeff is here."

"Oh, okay, then I'm comin down."

Or they'd say, "Oh let me talk to somebody." ... and then to somebody, "What are yous doin later on?"

"Oh, we're probably gonna meet and go to a movie. So come down now, have a couple of drinks and we'll come back after the movies."

When we were in there we were spendin money. Alan didn't cover charge. You came and went as you pleased and people were comin and goin, so he always made money.

Unfortunately, Alan had a very bad alcohol problem, and owning a bar you drink like crazy. Many a night I would go down there at eight or nine o'clock at night and I'd walk in and someone would be behind the bar giving away drinks. I'd say, "Where is Alan?"

"Oh, he's passed out over on the sofa."

I'd go, "Alan! Alan!" And I'd try to get him up. And I couldn't get him up.

Back at the bar, ... "All right, get the fuck from behind the bar. Alan told me to take over. Don't worry, I'll take care of the bar."

I would take care of the bar and I would close the bar and then put a blanket on Alan, get the keys out of his pocket and lock up for him.

In the mornin I'd go down there, "Alan, you can't do this shit, they're givin away liquor. It's like a big party. You can't do it."

But you couldn't tell him.

Or he'd go out with somebody and leave somebody tendin bar. He'd go out to dinner for three hours, come back with half a load on, go into the register, pull out a hundred dollars, go into the city and spend the night in the city drinkin, come back and drink more, bring people back with him, drink for nothin.

"Alan, you can't do this, you just can't do this!"

But that was Alan. Drink and party. But he had a good soul, a good heart and he never hurt anybody.

Alan owned that club Brazil for a good three years. Then he sold the bar to Nora. Nora had no personality and she was nasty to everybody. She would never buy back a drink. Usually they buy back every third drink in bars. If you buy two they give you one for free. It's the right way to run a bar. When my parents were bartending, the house always bought back, it was a given in a neighborhood bar. In gay bars, though, not so much, ... but with a bar on Staten Island, you gotta treat it like a neighborhood bar. You buy back.

Nora would charge admission to come in on a Saturday night...without having a show. She would have the jukebox goin on, she wouldn't hire a deejay. She wanted five or ten dollars to walk in the door because it was a gay bar. She would put out peanuts and potato chips and she would say, that's what you're payin for.

Now when you make a cover charge, people would say,

"What do I need this for? If I'm gonna pay a cover charge, I'll go to the city in fifteen minutes. There'll be boys dancin on the bar, there'll be a drag show, there'll be a disc jockey."

"You know what? We don't have to meet down there."

"We're gonna pay ten dollars to go into a place to stay for two or three hours, and then leave to go to Manhattan, and then when we want to come back, she wants to charge us again to come back?"

If you wanna come in again, you have to pay again. That was Nora's way. ...

It got to the point where we would get to the municipal parking lot a block away and stop there, and just stand around and chat and meet up with whoever. Somebody would show up with beer. Then the word got around that the parking lot in South Beach was a place for gay people to meet, and soon other people were turning up and hanging out as well. Being gay people, it wasn't long before they were cruising there at all hours. It became a scene in itself. Nora was furious, "Go down there and see if they're in the parking lot!" she would say to one of her flunkies. "Tell them to get over here!" But of course, we didn't go and the municipal parking lot became the new place to be seen on Staten Island. And with no entrance fee.

I only worked one show with Nora and she gypped me outta money. It was right after she took over. There were four of us doin the show, Norman Perkins, Carla Cupcake, myself and Booboo. We already had a show booked for New Year's Eve when she took over.

She said, "Well, you're still gonna do the New Year's Eve show?"

"Yeah, okay."

We went in. It was our usual hour show with an opening and a closing of the first half and an opening of the second half and a finale. In between, we did singles. It was New Years and we were gonna do two shows, one at ten o'clock and then another at one o'clock. We did the ten o'clock show and she came in and she paid us for the ten o'clock show, and she said, "I don't have enough money to pay you for the one o'clock show, so do that one for free."

I said, "I don't think so. What do you mean, you don't have enough money. You have a full house. You charge 40 dollars a couple to come in. You're givin them a cold buffet. They're drinkin like crazy, you're chargin for drinks. You don't have enough money to pay us? If you're not gonna pay us, we're not gonna do the show."

"Well, that's your prerogative. But you already have everything here. You're doin the same show over again. Why should I pay you a second time to do the same show over again!"

"Nora, this is the deal, we settled this a month ago. You wanted it."

And Norman ... "You fuckin sawed off dyke! Who the fuck do you think you're playin with? You're not gonna get a fuckin show.

I'm goin down there to tell my friends to leave right now. Who the fuck do you think you're dealin with?!"

Oh and he carried on terrible.

Alan was there and he said, "Oh, I'm so sorry,..."

And us, ... "Alan, don't worry about it. You have nothing to do with this at all, you're just here to support the bar. It's her bar and she knew all the money details. We discussed it and she agreed to it and now she's backin out. She's figurin, *you know what, they'll do it for nothin cause they did the first one and they don't want to disappoint people...* "

As we're carryin on up there about all this Norman goes downstairs, gets the microphone from the deejay and tells the whole club what's goin on and how Nora is upstair arguin with us.

We came downstairs, and she had lost probably thirty people who walked out. It was already after midnight and there were other clubs to go to. Everybody went down to Bayzie's and that's where we did shows from there on in, too.

When Alan bought the bar, he had to answer to the mob. It was an ongoing thing. Then when he sold it to Nora, he had to get permission from Ratz and the boys because they had a piece of the action. Nora also had to meet with them and they had to okay the sale and she had to okay the fact that she had to give them a piece of the action, because it was still a mob bar.

Of course, Nora got in and she would try, "Well I'm gonna skip a payment." Or this or that.

They'd call up Nathan Stoutmeyer and say, "Go down and talk to this bitch. Go down and talk to this cunt. Tell this cunt that she's not missin no payments. Or she'll be missin a bathroom. Because we'll tear the bathroom out one night and she'll have to pay to get it redone, because that's not in the contract. She's gotta take care of things."

Walter was the owner of the building. He rented out all the apartments above the bar. He would go down and say, "Nora, if you know what's good for ya ... I'm not threatenin ya, and they're not threatenin ya, they're just givin you a very peaceful bit of advice. Give them the money, they can make life miserable for you."

But I think there were a couple of times she didn't give in, and they did make life miserable for her. Then she did pay up, and then she was okay.

But before you knew it, she was out too. She was like, "I had enough of this shit." She sold it to Denise. By that time, she had run the bar down so badly, that nobody wanted to go there, no matter who owned it, so Denise couldn't make a go of it. After one year she sold that bar and she opened the Fire Loft up in Stapleton, a gay bar for a year and a half, if that. That was the end of the old Jack O'Clubs for good this time. Then somebody bought the building and tore it down.

19. HENRY

Nickie would call home and say, "I'm bringin somebody home for dinner, set an extra plate." ... and his mother would set an extra plate. And "somebody" would come in. Some of them were real doozies, like Henry.

Nickie was about 50 and Henry was about 25 and dumb as a rock. He was a nice enough guy, cute, great body, twinkle in his eye, but he was a little ditzy. You would imagine a fifty year old dating an eighteen year old girl. Lolita-ish, but on a boy it was really strange and although he wasn't in drag, he wasn't cross dressing, he was as effeminate as feminine could be. He had a heavy lisp when he talked and he was thin and slight. You looked at him and said, *oh my God, what's goin on with this one?*

We used to go out to eat together, and if the waiter would ask Henry first he would say, "Oh, I'm not ready yet." And they would go around the table and then Henry would say, "Oh, give me what he's havin!"

Then we realized, Henry cannot read.

He would say and do the most bizarre things. He would wear things like cut off midriff fishnet shirts and these short short shorts, skin skin tight, and he would show up for dinner at Nickie's family's house with this get-up on.

Marla, Nickie's sister would come in to have her hair done. "What was that get-up on Henry?"

Mario, Nickie's brother, would come in for a haircut that weekend and say, "What the fuck is up with Henry? He had a fishnet shirt on. My mother was lookin at him and my father said to him, 'Are you one of those male dancers or somethin?'

Henry said, 'No. What do you mean?'

And my father, 'Oh, nothin.'"

Henry was totally oblivious to anything, didn't realize that he was dressing a little risqué for an old Italian family. And Nickie would just eat like everything was okay. Nickie didn't talk, nothin said, old school. Some of Nickie's favorite phrases were, *The ox is slow but the earth is patient; The less said the better.*

But one look from Nickie would say a thousand things. Somebody would say somethin out of line and Nickie would just look.

Oops, he's givin you that look, you'd better stop! Walk away, cause it's not good.

One of his boyfriends once said somethin out of line and he cracked him in the shoulder with a two by four. He was doin some contracting for me down in the basement and he had a two by four in his hand. Whack! Whoa!

That became one of our jokes.

"Watch out! Is that a two by four situation?"

Watch out, he'll get a two by four!

One time Nickie called me up and said, "What are you doin tonight?"

I said, "I'm makin dinner, why don't you come over for dinner."

He says, "Okay, we'll be over for dinner."

"I guess you're bringin Henry."

"Yeah."

Cause he wouldn't even tell me.

"Yeah, I'm gonna go pick him up."

"All right. Pick up somethin for dessert."

"All right."

He picked up a chocolate cream pie and he called me up and said, "Is that good?"

"Yeah, a chocolate cream pie is fine."

"All right, fine."

He put the chocolate cream pie on the seat next to him. Then he picked up Henry. When Henry got in the car Nickie said, "Here, put this on your lap, so it doesn't shake. It's a chocolate cream pie."

"All right."

So Henry put it on his lap and said, "What's the chocolate cream pie for?"

"We're goin over to Freddie and Leon's for dinner."

"Oh, again?"

Nickie looked. But Henry was totally oblivious, as usual.

A couple of minutes went by.

Henry said, "I really didn't want to go out tonight, I really didn't want to go there. Why can't we go out and have somethin to eat in the diner?"

"Cause I already told them we're comin over."

"Well, I don't wanna go over. Why can't we go have somethin in the diner? There's no reason why we can't go to the diner. Just call them up and tell them that we're not comin over."

"He already set a place."

"Well, so what? We don't have to go over. We can go to the diner."

Nickie pulled over to the side of the road. "Gimme the cake."

He took the cake and BAM! He slammed him right in the face, the carton and everything exploded.

"Get out of the fuckin car, now."

Henry opened up the car and he started screamin, and he ran.

Nickie came up the stairs. There was chocolate cream pie on his shorts, on his legs and his sandals, and even on his bald head.

"What the hell is all over you?"

"Chocolate cream pie."

"What do you mean?"

"Gimme the vacuum cleaner and a bucket."

"Why?"

"There's chocolate cream pie all over the car."

I went down to the car, it looked like the box and the chocolate cream pie exploded. He hit the kid so hard with the box, all you seen was pieces of chocolate and cream and pie and cake all splattered in every part of the car.

So we replaced the two by four with the chocolate cream pie. Is this a two by four situation? No, it's more a chocolate cream pie situation!

20. EARTH PACT

The first year of Earth.

People usually become attached to different elements. I was always very attached to Earth. Even at the youngest age. People used to say somethin like, "What are you doin' playin in the dirt like that?"

But I was thinking, "I'm playing in the earth, I'm not playing in the dirt, I'm playing in the *Earth*."

It's an organic, living being, the Earth, and so is the Sun, and so is Water and so is Fire for that matter. It's all got its energy to it.

Leon was very attached to Fire. His pagan name was Mithras, the god of fire. I was Myrddin who was Merlin before he was Merlin. I was like the young Merlin.

When I did my Earth pact, I was like ah, I'm Earth, I'm all Earth. I arrogantly said, There's nobody else that's more earth than I am! There's no point in even doing this pact. I'm at my own element. So I'm gonna go out and have a good time, I'm not gonna learn anything. *I'm Earth!*

So the first year of Earth we went to the Poconos. We used to go up to a resort called, "High Above the Poconos" and we would get a big cabin for the night for all of us with a big fireplace. The day before we were doing our pact, we went out to pick places that we wanted to go to when we set out on our own. That's how it's done: you're together, you open circle, a particular circle to bless you for what's to come in the pact and then each individual person goes out and does their own pact separately. Then you come back together and you close the circle.

It was winter and it was going to be cold out and I was so worried about Carlos because he was such a city boy. He couldn't even light a match; he had to have a lighter. What are we gonna do with Carlos? Poor Carlos, he's gonna get hurt out here!

So I was worried, and I was like, "Oh, Carlos, you hafta..."

"Oh, Carlos, no you don't...."

"Oh, are you okay, Carlos?"

"Oh, you don't ..."

"I'm fine! I'm fine! I'm fine!" he would say. Or: "All right, all right! You know?"

"Leon, you're okay?"

"I'm fine, I'm fine."

I said to myself, *I'm goin into a cave.* I found a cave. *I'm gonna build a fire in the cave, I'm gonna set up my firewood, so that I'm nice and warm and I'm gonna take plenty of cayenne before I do pact, so that I'm warm inside. I'm gonna dress really really well to keep warm, so I know I'm gonna be so comfortable. I'm gonna do it right on the edge of a brook.* There was a beautiful brook with a pile of big boulders that you would climb up to get to this cave right in the mountainside. It was a small cave, maybe ten by ten and ten foot high. *That's where I'm gonna do my pact and it's gonna be so easy.* I put my matches there that first day and everything else to start my fire, and I had my specially infused wine to do my pact with, everything set up perfectly.

It was a rainy night. It was so chilly that we started out with Antonia to open circle in the cabin rather than outside. Then we walked in the woods by ourselves to do our thing. There was a big hill that we had to climb up to go into where the mountains were. We climbed up this big hill that was all dirt now, the grass had died back and so it was basically just pounded down earth. I went off to the right to where I was going and they went off to the left. It started to snow and I said, oh my goodness, snow, this is wonderful. We should have snow on a nice winter pact!

I got to the brook, climbed up the stones to the cave. I got in the cave, opened circle. Tried to light my fire. I had twenty matches in the matchbook, they kept on blowing out on me. On the last match I got down on the ground, burning my hand to get to the fire. I lit the fire finally, really nicely but the fire got too big. It was so hot in that cave, between the cayenne and the clothes I had on. I had to take all these clothes off, I was down to a tee shirt. The top of the cave had moisture that had frozen so now it started raining in the cave from the heat I had created. I'm soakin wet and I'm hot, and there's cold water fallin. So I struggled down to get water from the stream for my pact. I'm struggling down the rocks and I fall and I go into the stream, almost waist high in this freezing cold water. I crawl back up to the cave and I get into the cave and I'm listening and I'm saying *Oh my God, I hear drums.*

I'm at the edge of the cave, *Those are drums, I'm hearin.*
bumbumbumbumbum
This is definitely not thunder, this is drums! I'm hearin drums!

Now I'm startin to get afraid, *this is crazy,* I says, *I'm closin circle, I'm gettin out of here, I'm scared, everything is going wrong.*

I closed circle, I did what I had to do, I did my pact and I was just thinking, *Please help me through this, I'm realizin I ain't shit, in the bigger scheme of things I am a little bitty person I am not Earth. I have a lot to learn about the Earth. I'm sorry. Dad, please take me home, will ya? I'll be a good pagan!*

I got outside and now it started sleeting. I got to the top of the hill and thought, *Thank God, it's all over now, there's the cabin down at the end of the hill that I have to walk down. No problem at all.* I took two steps and I fell on my ass and slid all the way down the hill right down to the cabin door. I got up and took six steps. I went to open up the cabin door, and Antonia opened up and she said, "I guess that'll teach you, won't it? You got kicked in your ass."

21. ROBIN

Robin and I met when I met Leon. I met Robin down the beach on the boardwalk. He says, "How ya doin?"

"Okay. I'm actually waitin for somebody. I know that's an old story, I'm waitin for somebody."

"Who you waitin for?" he says.

"Somebody I met a couple of days ago. His name's Leon."

"Oh I know Leon!" he says.

"Oh yeah?"

"Yeah!"

I says, "Very nice."

"Yeah, he *is* very nice!"

It turned out that he fooled around with Leon also, and I fooled around with Leon.

We ended up becoming good friends and Robin even became part of the coven. We stayed good friends all through life, which wasn't very long for Robin, unfortunately. Very quiet, lovable, not aggressive in life. His father was the owner of four or five of those modeling schools. His father was hardly ever home and his mother was a very take-control woman. Very cold, very by-the-rules.

Robin used to laugh and say, "She drives me crazy, she drives me crazy. She's gotta have the snow piled up a certain way. It's gotta be on two sides of the steps going up to the house, because there are two bay windows, on each side; so all the snow has to be piled in front of the bay windows, a foot below the bay windows, only from bay window to bay window. All the snow from the driveway and the sidewalk all has to go there."

"But ma, what's the difference? It's all gonna melt anyway."

"No! It doesn't look neat! It's gotta be neat!"

Meanwhile, Robin would put on two different socks. He just didn't care. He didn't know, he didn't care.

Robin, being the loving, silly soul that he was, would come to circle and we would have to reprimand him. He would kiss us hello and I would say, "Robin, were you smokin weed? I can smell it on ya."

He'd say, "Yeah, I had a little bit before I came."

"Robin, you know you're not supposed to partake of any substance whatsoever prior to circle."

We even try not to have caffein, only because during circle you're giving yourself to the gods. You don't want to give them something that's tainted. During circle you're opening yourself, so that the gods or spirits of anybody or anything can come within you. It's called an invocation to take a spirit in you. You can't have a spirit come into a body that has a foreign substance in it. A spirit doesn't know how to take to something like that.

But Robin would always be, "Oh, I just smoked a little bit o' weed. I met so and so, and he took out a joint and I just took a hit off a it."

"Robin, you can't do that!"

"All right. I'll go make coffee and I'll put the cake out for after circle and you do circle without me."

He would never be angry and we would never be angry because you couldn't be angry with Robin.

He was a lovable guy and a little sex doll, too. He was always down the beach, in the bathhouses. At this time we started to find out about AIDS. I said, "Robin, you really need to be careful."

"No, I'm careful."

"You're doin too much. You have to be careful when you go to the baths."

"I always do a little prayer to the goddess to protect me."

"Robin, you can't pray to the goddess to protect you, and then go and have sex with seventeen people. It's just not the right thing to do. Say, you sit home and you pray because you need money desperately. You need to walk out and at least buy a lottery ticket, because the gods have to have a way to give you that money you're prayin for. Look for a job - that's your opening for the gods to do the right thing for you. Magic works in mysterious ways, but you gotta work the magic. You can't just pray to the goddess that you're not gonna catch AIDS and then go to the baths three times a week. It's just not nice. They're gonna be very angry at you."

He was twenty-eight or twenty-nine and he would roll along from day to day, not workin much. He had two or three or four jobs, stupid little things. He had a job with a florist for two or three weeks. He stayed out late and got into work late and they fired him.

"Where were you?" I asked him.

"Oh, I was at the boardwalk. I was hangin out with Kenny and Vinnie and Joey. We were just drinkin and laughin and havin a good time. We ended up goin home two or three o'clock in the mornin and I couldn't get up for work. I showed up at work two hours late again, they fired me. Ah, so what, I'll find another job."

He was never like, oh, I'm a failure, I don't know what I'm gonna do. His parents were loaded and they could afford to put him through things. He didn't ask for crazy things, he didn't have his own car. He didn't need it, he didn't want it. He would call up and say to me, "Oh, you wanna go out to Manhattan tonight? C'mon let's go. You have the car, yeah, let's go."

22. INVOCATION OF PAN

I was the last one to get back to the cabin that night of Earth Pact. We all sat down to finish circle, me in my soaking wet clothes. I had been so worried about everyone else but now I could see that Leon was perfect. He had done everything wonderful. I looked at Carlos. He was as happy as a lark. And me? The Earth had laughed its ass off at me.

We would do the wine blessing, the bread blessing, we would thank the spirits and then we would close the circle. After that, it would be time to laugh and reflect and talk about what happened. You don't do that right away. But after the circle is closed you can laugh, you can drink, you can partake of substances.

We sat down in circle again. I realized I was being touched by an invocation. An invocation is when a spirit enters you. I felt this tremendous amount of chills and warmth at the same time. My head started to spin and visions came into my head. The vision of the god Pan. Pan is the god of the forest, the keeper of the animals, half man and half animal. He is the god that says although you are man you are still animal, you're still a bear, a wolf, a goat, a cow, a horse.

With that comes a camaraderie, a brotherhood, all of these animals are my family, the trees, the sky, the earth, the water are all my family. As this vision was building, this great god was evolving, not at all like the Pan that I had in my imagination, a happy, funny cloven footed god running around drinking, playing, making merry constantly. No, Pan was this extremely huge goat with man parts to it. This goat was sad and crying and full of sympathy for the world and the animals around it. This god came within me so that I could feel all of these things. It was very empowering, I was that gigantic spirit of Pan and I had these obligations as well as all these attributes of the entire forest. I stopped to think, yes, your ass was kick by the great god Pan, the father of the forest. ... and yet at the same time, after he kicked your ass, he held on to you and he hugged you and he said to you, *it's okay.*

You are me and I am you and we're gonna get through this together. We need to take care of business, we need to be one with each other, but not with the arrogance that you had when you stepped out, but with the respect, the love and the knowledge of being with the Earth ... or I'll kick your ass again!

23. ROBIN'S END

He wanted to go to California and he wanted to do flower arrangements. So he went to California to get a job with some flower company. He came back from there HIV positive. At that time, Leon was already diagnosed HIV positive too.

It was about eight or ten months before Leon died that Robin got really sick. He started getting dementia. It was a sad thing. Robin would walk over to my house, get there and not know where he was. I would take him home and his mother would say, "He was in bed under the covers and I came in to give him lunch and he was gone.'

He would go out the back door.

He became bedridden and I would go over to see him at the house. His mother was like, *keep the blinds down, don't let anybody know...*

Then he went into the hospital and one day I went to see him and his eyes were completely open and his mother and father were there.

His mother said, "He's not in a coma, but he's not able to talk. He can hear but he can't even close his eyes."

She closed his eye and it popped back open again. He couldn't move his fingers but he was conscious.

She went on. "You know, out of all my children, he was the most lovable and caring. He would walk up to me and say, I'm goin out, I'll see you later, ma ... And for no reason, he would reach around and kiss me on the cheek.

I don't kiss my children.

I would say why does he do that? It's so nice of him to do. But I would never reciprocate and I would never start doin it. He would give me a hug and I wouldn't even hug him back because *I don't hug my children,* that's the way I am. I'm gonna miss that love, because he wasn't afraid to show affection, even though I never showed affection to him or to any of my children."

His father said, "When I first found out he was gay, I said, why can't you be like your brother? Why can't you be like your sister, why can't you go to college?"

His sister was a pharmacist, and his brother went to college, a professional.

"Why can't you be straight?" Then his father turned to us. "But you know I could never be half the man that Robin was. Robin never whimpered about any of this. He never said *why me?* I never seen him cry. God knows if it was me, I probably would have sat down and cried myself to death. But Robin never cried. He was more of a man than I could ever hope to be."

We looked over at Robin and there was a little tear comin out of his eyes. We were like wow, look at that. He listened to every word that we were sayin, and he listened to the affirmation that his parents said about him.

It was no more than three hours later that he died.

He stuck around for that reason; he needed the affirmation of his parent. Or maybe it was the opposite way around. Maybe he needed to teach them. Maybe he came back from a different life specifically to teach them how to be warm and giving. To teach his father how to be tolerant, to not want more than anything else, and to teach his mother how to show love.

He was here to live, to love, to teach people simple little things. He wasn't here for much or for long, he wasn't here to be a go getter, to be the owner of a company, to be the best whatever. He was just a little boy in a grown up soul. We had our times together and those times were good.

24. CLIPS OF NICKIE

The first time the three of us, Nickie, Leon and me, went to Puerto Rico together, we shared the room. Nickie would take one bed and Leon and I would take the other bed. Leon and I would go to bed early and Nickie would go roamin the streets - Ashford Avenue, where all the guys hung out. Nickie rented a car and he would roll up and down Ashford Avenue. Honk honk! Hey! Pa' aqui pa' aqui!

And the boy would come over.

C'mon, get in the car!

Rapraprap on the door and Nickie would open it up and there's Nickie with some guy. He would pick up the dregs of humanity, all these hustlers. Leon and I would be sleepin with one hand on the lamp to hit the guy if he ever started trouble, ...but there was never any trouble. Nickie was good for one or two a night, every single night. Drop off one, pick up another one. Two or three hours later there would be another one. Back in the room again! Nickie was insatiable.

*****

I was with Leon about a year. We were livin together. Nickie calls me up and says, "What are you doin tonight?"

"Nothin."

"Tell Leon we're goin out to dinner in Manhattan."

"All right, what's the occasion?"

"Nothin. I'll meet you at Boysbarn after you close up the shop. We'll go have dinner in Manhattan. I got a surprise for ya."

"All right."

He comes by around six or seven o'clock.

"We're goin to Chinatown."

"All right, that's nice."

We go into the restaurant and we're sittin there.

So I says, "What's the surprise?"

"The surprise should be here any minute."

So what happens? Who comes walkin in? Dick Sweet, from the bar! Dick Sweet that went to Florida. I says, "I can't believe it!" This had to be like fifteen years after I seen him. He comes walkin in, baldish on top, gained about forty pounds. Not lookin good at all.

I said, "Wow, it's good to see you!"

"Yeah, yeah," he says. "Who's this?"

"This is Leon."

"Oh, he's with you?"

"Yeah."

"Oh, I thought he was with Nickie. I thought Nickie was up to his old tricks. I see you picked up where Nickie left off. He's a little young for you, isn't he?"

"No, he's not that young for me."

"He's a little young for ya."

"Well, he's a whole lot older than you were when you were with Nickie. Or when I was with Nickie."

"Yeah, yeah, all right."

And Leon was not courteous whatsoever, because he knew all the stories about Dick Sweet. Dick was a contractor and he had come in from Florida for a week or two to visit his mother in New Jersey.

Later, after Dick left, Nickie said to me, "How do you feel about him?"

"What do you mean how do I feel about him? How do you feel about him?"

"Ah, No me! No me!"

I says, "No me!"

"He lost his appeal, huh?"

"Totally. No more sweet tooth for me."

The both of us had been head over heels in love with that boy. No me! No me either!

That was the last time we seen Dick Sweet or ever heard of him. He didn't age very well at all. The spark was gone, my heart didn't go pitter patter no more.

*****

Nickie used to have to park his car in the Village to pick up his truck and do his rounds. Then come five o'clock he would drop the truck off in the meatpacking district and pick up his car again. Before he'd come home he would make his own rounds: the Village, Fifty-third and Third, see what he could acquire. He wasn't one to pick up hustlers and pay but he would pick them up and take them to dinner. Paying for sex was against his morals, but doin like he done for me so many years before, paying for dinner, getting them clothes, setting them up in an apartment, was more acceptable.

Nickie once picked up a kid named Josh at the cruising area at Fifty-third and Third. That entire block was an area where hustlers would pick up johns. There were a few hustler bars there, like Cowboys & Cowgirls and the Townhouse. Josh was a hustler. He worked Cowboys & Cowgirls and he worked the street. Nickie brought him to Boysbarn and he had the smelliest feet. We had a habit of taking off our shoes when we came into the house. Nickie would come in and take off his shoes and the kid would take off his shoes. We always had people in the house, it was the get together house and the stink was so bad that people would look around like *what the hell is goin on? Who the hell's feet? That is horrible!*

It got to the point where Josh would come in and, "Uh, uh, you're stayin over?"

"Yeah."

"Go take a shower."

"No, I don't need a shower."

"No no, if you're comin in, you're comin off the streets, you're takin a shower. That's it."

"No, no."

And finally:

"Your feet stink! So if you're takin off your shoes..."

He wasn't proud, he was a street boy, who knows how long he kept his shoes on?

Dumb as a rock but street smart, Josh looked like he would pick your pocket and stab you at the same time. But he was a good kid and Nickie kept him under control. Nickie read him the riot act so there was never anything missin, Josh wasn't gonna play any games, because he knew Nickie would have him drawn and quartered. Nickie took him to the right places, showed him around, and Josh was cool. He lasted a few months, then someone said,

"Nickie, c'mon let's all go to the Hamptons for the weekend."

Nickie was good friends with Alan Brazil who was now caretaking for someone in Southampton after he sold the business to

Nora. Nickie asked Josh to come along for the weekend. It was horrendous. They had a fight there. Nickie drove him back to the city and dropped him off in the village and said, "Go your own way." And that was the end of Josh.

*****

Nickie and I lasted a good long time. I have dreams all the time about him and his family. Being pagan we had a close bond. We had past life regressions that we had together. There was definitely an entwinement. There was a specialness when I first met Nickie and there was a specialness that we had all through our relationship. It came in a full circle ... him helping me grow up and later on, me being an adult, ... and then that respect that we had where we were almost equals. Then later on in life when I became the parent to Leon, and Nickie was the grandfather.

We would go out with coven, eight of us going out for dinner together before circle, and the check would come and Nickie would grab the check. That's only gonna happen once or twice. We would go out for dinner and I would go over to the waitress and say, "You make sure you give me the check." She would give me the check.

"All right, here it is, right here"

"What are you doin?" Nickie would say.

"You know what, it's twenty dollars each."

And that's the end of the situation. "You're not pickin up the check. It's not happenin." And I said to everybody else, "He's not doin it, this is not fair."

He's a good guy and he can be abused very easily and I'm not gonna have anybody abusin him. We go out, we go out Dutch.

Nickie and I and Leon would go out and I would grab the check myself.

Nickie you did this all too often in the past. I can never repay you for all the checks that you've grabbed the bill for me. And it's not about that no more. Now it's about me takin care of my own, and me sayin thank you to you.

*****

When Nickie retired he went to Florida to an assisted living community. But he still did everything his way. He had lots of really good jewelry, he used to collect Hummels and Lladro. He had a lot of antique furniture. His sisters in law all said, *oh, when you die Nickie, I want this, oh when you die I want that. Who are you leavin your jewelry to? I want this, I want that.*

"The bastards, they're like vultures. They're always around, they want this, they want that. If you ask them for help for somethin, you're never gonna get it, but they want everything. You know what? Nobody's gettin nothin."

And he'd have that sneaky laugh.

When he died, I said, "Did he leave a will?"

"Will? He didn't have anything left."

"What do you mean?"

"The last two years he was alive he sold everything he had. Everything! There wasn't a thing left - no jewelry, especially. Even the condominium he sold to his friend, Paul, a real estate agent. He sold it to him with a contract that said Nickie was allowed to live there until he died.

Paul also collected antiques and he bought a lot of Nickie's things. What Paul didn't buy they put ads in the newspapers and he cleaned out his entire apartment, everything, there wasn't a thing left. I looked at that man in his casket and I said to his brother, does it not look like he's got a grin on his face? Because he did it his way. He spent every penny that he had. He lived, lived, lived until he died.

25. THE HANDFASTING

While the coven was together I wouldn't even think about a Halloween party or going out on Halloween night. It would be painful not to be together for that particular night. Pagan people always had a respect for the dead and on that night the veil between the spirit world and the living world is at its thinnest. Spirits can cross over and tap in, it is the easiest time for them to come back. When you do circles on Halloween night, spirits come to you and wonderful things can happen.

Leon and I were together for a long enough time and Antonia said, "Don't you think its time for a hand-fasting for you two?"

A pagan marriage, a hand-fasting.

So we sat down and we started thinking about, well who would we invite? ... and where would we have it? ... carefully writing down every little detail that we wanted said and done for the hand-fasting. It was set for about four months from this particular date.

We went out to do our second year of Water Pact. We just didn't have enough time to go away, so we decided to do it across the street at Mount Manresa. there was enough space for four or five of us to spread out and each do our own circle and then come together with Antonia.

I went up above the grotto in the woods, and Leon went someplace else and Carlos and Nickie went other places. After my pact was over, I decided to wander through the woods. It was slightly chilly, typical October, rainy, and you could hear the rain all hitting the leaves, a little bit of thunder in the background. I started walking around in the woods, and boom! I bumped into Leon.

I said, "Are you done with your pact?"

I didn't want to interrupt him.

"Oh yeah," he said, "I just felt like walking around afterwards."

We hugged and kissed and we said, *you now what? This should be our hand-fasting. Nobody else should be here.* We decided to make our vows and do our hand-fasting there. And then we made love right there to consummate it.

When we did our handfasting, the rain was upon us and our emotions were a part of the rain, a part of the water. Water is the element of emotion. When we cry, water comes from our eyes, when we have sex, water carries our seed.

When we came back to the house, circle was still opened up and Antonia was there and everyone else was sitting in circle. We stepped into circle and she just looked at us and said, "You couldn't wait could you?"

I said, "Wait for what?"

"Your hand-fasting, You did it, didn't you?"

We had made all the preparations and it all was beautiful on paper, what flowers we were going to use and what this that and the other thing. But you know what? It just didn't belong to anyone else but us. There should be no big deal about it. There should be nothing except the two us and the god and goddess to bless over us.

26. THE SHOP IN ST. GEORGE

I had that shop in New Dorp that I bought from Lucille, right off Hylan Boulevard, for ten years. I seen this salon in St. George was up for sale. I remembered it because I went to McKee High School and I used to walk past it and my friend Marsha who went to McKee with me used to work there as a shampoo girl. Julian Foster owned it, Foster's Coiffures. Bob Julian was the ultimate flaming fairy hairdresser. Six foot three, bleached blond hair with a big deep wave in it. He was fiftyish, very thin, very tall, very sleek, he always spoke properly. He used to go to the Mayfair all the time.

I contacted the lady and she didn't want much for it. The people that were there running it prior to me ran out on six months rent and just disappeared and left everything there. So I said to her, "I'll give you a thousand dollars for the furniture."

She said, "Great. I'll take it."

I gave her the thousand dollars and we opened the next day.

Leon had just gotten out of hairdressing school and he was working with me in New Dorp and I hired a black hairdresser named DeVonne that worked for "Black Hair Is," a very chic chain of salons in Manhattan. They had fifteen salons and hired all Black hairdressers and he was one of their best. He came to this salon and he rented the basement apartment from me as well with his boyfriend, a skinny little white boy. We would close up the New Dorp salon at nine o'clock at night and we would close the other salon at nine also. We'd walk in there at nine o'clock on Friday night and there would be sixteen Black girls in there waitin to get their hair done.

"You'd better learn, it's CP time."

I said, "What's CP time?"

"Colored People Time."

He told me, you know, Black people were always like chauffeurs, maids, cooks. So, when they said that the wedding starts at seven p.m., it could start at eight thirty, nine thirty, ten o'clock even, depending on when everybody got off of work, because you had to finish up your job before you could leave. They didn't work from nine to five, they worked until dinner was over. If someone wanted a second portion, you stayed another twenty minutes before you could clean up. If somebody had more of a mess in their room, you had to clean it and then you'd go home.

So now we all got used to working on CP time. DeVonne would be doing hair in there till one o'clock in the morning, making a huge amount of money, charging these people a hundred and fifty dollars for a hairdo. I would go in there and I would bring Leon in there because we lived together. And Leon would say, "DeVonne, do you want me to shampoo for ya?" And he'd shampoo them. He'd put a conditioner on, bring em back, take rollers out for him.

It couldn't last. Six months into this whole thing, of him working for me, DeVonne lost his mind. He lost his mind in the shop. Somebody called me from next door and said, "You'd better get down here quick, because we're afraid that your window is gonna break or somethin. Somethin is gonna happen, they're havin a big fight."

"Who?"

"The guy that works for you and his boyfriend."

I go down there and the boyfriend threw somethin against the window, tryin to break the window. DeVonne went out and he got the boyfriend and he beat the boyfriend in the street, kicked him in the stomach, left him in the gutter.

I said, "What the hell is goin on?"

"It's none a your business!"

"Whoa, back up a bit. I own the salon!"

"You own the salon but I do all the work! I'm leavin! Fuck you and fuck the salon! I'm leavin and I'm movin outta your house!"

He was out of his mind. He walked out and there were all customers there. I says, "What am I gonna do?"

Leon said, "Don't worry about it, I'll take care of it."

I said, "What are you gonna do?"

"I can do their hair, don't worry about it."

"You never did Black hair in your life!"

"I been watchin him do it for six months. It's easy, there's nothin to do."

He started turnin out heads, and the women that were there were sayin, "If DeVonne comes back next week, we don't want him. We want Leon."

So I says, "Leon it looks like you're running the salon."

I came home that night and they were fightin in the driveway. The two of them, skinny wiry things, were throwin each other in the street, screamin at each other. They were bloody messes, the both of them killin each other with sticks and rocks. You had to see them fight, it was wild. I had to call the police to break it up.

The policeman said, "Who do you want to stay?"

"It's not up to me who stays, they both rented the apartment. I don't give a shit, but I can't have this all night."

They both left. DeVonne later opened up a place on Bay Street. It lasted six months or a year and then that closed. As crazy as a loon.

Leon stayed in St. George from there on in. He was this white hairdresser doin Black hair and the girls were lovin him and they were tellin their friends about him. In another three months, Leon was booked Monday through Saturday. Sixteen hours a day he was doing hair. He had two people in helpin him, doing what he had been doin for DeVonne, and he was doin better work than DeVonne did.

We went to a Black hair show because we wanted to see more about Black hair. We looked for Revlon relaxers, and they said, we're really sorry but the artist that's gonna show the relaxer just called in. He's stuck on the highway and he can't make it in. We're gonna have to cancel the showing of this Revlon relaxer.

Before we left the house that day, Leon had said, "I would love to be a platform artist."

So I walked over to the guy that was heading up the Revlon showing and I said, "I have someone that works for me that's very, very good. If you want him to take over, he can do his best at showing the product."

"Yeah, I guess so."

I says, "Leon come here."

The guy says, "He's white!"

I said, "Yeah, I noticed."

"He can't do Black hair, he's white."

"Yes, he can. That's all we do is Black hair."

He got up on the stage and he did fantastic. So fantastic that they offered him a job and he worked for Revlon as a platform artist from there on in. The year that he died he was supposed to be doing Beverly Johnson and Iman's hair, the platform work for their photos. It was Revlon's division of Black hair, called Revlon's Special Markets, Black products for Black hair. Leon was the only white guy out of 370 Black hairdressers that worked for the Revlon Special Markets division. He would go on stage with blond hair, green eyes, White Russian. What's he doin up there with these Black women?

And he would just knock them over. He was fantastic and everybody that worked with him loved him.

27. FRAGMENTS OF LEON

Even toward the end with Leon, it brought so much comfort to him and to me to be in a spiritual place that we were very sure of. Anybody that is in a situation where they are terminally ill, I pray and hope that they would have some kind of spiritual path in front of them. We certainly did, and Leon followed that path to complete fullness, and he would say things to me about the things that he would see, the places he would go in his travels before he passed. It was another one of those gifts that he gave to me, to be able to see. It's not a bad place, death, it's a place that's welcoming and beautiful and not to be afraid of. Passing is a natural turn of the wheel.

Winter is the time of Earth, the time of the crone. There really is no death, there is just the crone, the old one, the wise one, and from that point of winter you go into spring, the time of the child, rebirth, the newness, the magic. so when you are in that time of Earth and you realize that this is the end, it's not really the end, its only the last spoke of the wheel before it turns back in again to the child. Everything is just one living creature that constantly evolves.

So you look on life as being a constant moving cycle. I seen Leon come into that in the very end. Although his own age was so young, I seen him become the crone. He could no longer walk, he no longer had any hair on his body whatsoever, and he had that wisdom, he had that fire in his green eyes. He understood far more than I understood because he was so much closer than I was. He cycled very quickly. Spring, Summer, Fall, Winter ... Child, Dancer, Parent, Crone.

Do I think the crones helped Leon pass? My goodness, yeah. His grandmother came to him, there's no doubt about it. Antonia was there with her grandmother who had passed. All the circles that we did for him helped him more and more: for him to seek guidance, for him to see clearly without fear. He went through it phenomenally. Even at the end, people would look, his nurse Donna would come in and say, "You look at him, I have so many clients that are all dying with AIDS, some of it is really horrible to look at, the transition of what they were and what they've become. They'll show me pictures of what they looked like a year and a half ago and you say, oh my God, a young, strong, muscular man in a bathing suit, now he looks livid, haggard, just sickly horrible... "

Leon seemed to have gone from what he was to a young Buddha. He was skinny, seventy something pounds, there was nothing left to him, but his skin glowed, there was this beautiful tone to his skin, and his eyes just blazed, they shined, big like ET, but green and sparkling, and not a hair on his head or his eyebrows or his lashes. Yet, he had this big smile. He had this inner glow, like pregnant women have sometimes? He had this inner glow of peace and love. People would look at him and say he just looks so beautiful in an entirely different light, not sexy beautiful, just beautiful.

It's a wonderful thing to be able to tap into your strength and ask for the strength of all the ages, instead of just giving it up to a priest or a nun or to fate. Take everything that's been learned by all these brilliant people in the past and add it to yourself. You have every right to that, every right to become your own priest, and not to be a sheep looking for a shepherd.

28. CARLOS' END

Carlos lived in Manhattan. Antonia the high priestess lived on Staten Island with her son Kevin at her mother's house.

When Carlos decided he wanted to learn more about paganism, Antonia said that's terrific.

When Leon and I decided to become pagan, we met Carlos a week later for dinner and he said, "I'm really interested in this, can I sit in on a class?" He did and he said, "I definitely want to be a part of this."

We called it the covenant of four: Antonia, Leon and me and Carlos. We called it that for the longest time, with Nickie just on the outside. There's always a coven of thirteen but we were so close, no one could break their way in. They just couldn't fit. It was like the quarters: North, South, East, West; or maybe Summer, Spring, Fall and Winter, but it was really Antonia, Leon, me and Carlos.

Being very close with a high priestess creates a bond, being gay and working with a high priestess is an oddity, because the bond becomes a love affair, though not necessarily sexual. Your high priest and your high priestess become your mother and your father, your lover, your best friend, husband, your wife, your brother, your sister. They become all of those things. That's why there are only thirteen people in a coven, because the bond becomes so tight and so close. That is also why sky clad worshiping is done a lot. "Sky clad" means you are totally naked. Because you have nothing to hide, nothing to enhance, nothing to desire, nothing to be ashamed of. You are just completely raw to your fellow coven members. Sky clad is not a sexual thing. Many people think that once circle is done you dance and it's a mad wild orgy. Unfortunately, that's not the way it is.

Becoming that close, it seemed that Carlos and Antonia connected. Carlos had a very good job at Bell Telephone. He said to Antonia, "Come to Manhattan, live at my apartment, bring your son Nevin, and he can go to school at the UN. I'll pay for the whole thing. I want to take on Nevin as my heir, as my protege. I want to do for him what you can't do for him and I want to have someone that I can say I helped along."

They went in.

... Later on there was a big falling out and Antonia left Manhattan with Nevin and there was crying and carrying on. Carlos was pissed off at everybody, and we found out that there was a love affair going on. Although he was gay and he was into lots of kinky stuff, he was carryin on with Antonia. They fell in love with each other. She was tolerant to all his sexual behavior, but something along the line went bad. We never got the whole story ... we never got no story from Carlos because Carlos completely stopped talking to everybody in the coven, assuming that everybody was mad at him.

Antonia went out and she maxxed out the credit card that he gave her to use because she wanted to hurt him as much as she possibly could. She bought anything and everything until he put a stop on it. "That way, he'll never talk to me again because I want him out of my life completely. I am so angry at him."

That cut Carlos off completely from our friendship.

When Leon became HIV positive and got sick, we sent word to one of Carlos' close friends, Linda, that used to come to circle. She used to also come in to have her hair done by Leon. So although Carlos was not talking to any of us, Linda still came over to the salon, but she wouldn't tell us anything about Carlos.

She said, Carlos has forbidden me to talk about him. I told him that I'm comin here, and that I hope he doesn't expect that to stop. I want to get my hair done by Leon and I still love Fred and everybody that's there. I won't go to circle any longer, because I did that with him, but I still want to say hello to everybody.

"That's fine," he said, "but I want absolutely no conversation about me whatsoever! If they say, we want to know somethin about Carlos, you walk away from them. Whatever happens, if I'm havin a birthday party, you don't say anything. You leave me out of the conversation, like neither one of you ever knew me!"

That's the way Carlos was. Strong willed bitch. And that's pretty much the way Antonia was, too. So, at that point, when Leon got really sick, we sent word with Linda that Leon was sick.

He never came by. When Leon died, he never came by. We left word that we were having a memorial and he never came by. Two or three months after Leon died, Linda came in and said, "Carlos passed away last night."

"What are you talkin about?"

"He was HIV positive, and he didn't want anybody to know about it. He forbidded me from tellin you. I've been taking care of him, feeding him the last couple of months because he wouldn't go to the hospital. He had a nurse that would come in for him and he finally passed away."

I was devastated. No wonder he didn't show up for Leon. He was sick.

She said, "Yeah, for the memorial service he was already very sick. He was paralyzed, he was in bed, couldn't get out. There was nothin he could do. I said to him many, many times, can I tell them? And he said no, absolutely not. You tell them after I'm gone."

So there it was. He didn't want anybody to know anything. He didn't want his parents to know about his paganism, and he didn't want his coven to know about his family. He didn't want the people at his job to know about his sexuality, and he didn't want the people involved in his sexuality to know about any of the above. "Don't tell my parents that I have pneumonia! Don't tell my co-workers I'm in the hospital! Don't tell my friends that I have AIDS!" He kept his life so compartmentalized that he made the same mistake that Ralph had made, and kept everyone at a distance.

He was my longest best friend, yet he had cut me and everyone else who cared about him out of one of the most important times of his life, his passing.

PART 4
AN EVOLVING RAIN

29. ALL THE YOUNG GUIDOS

Becoming friends with Mario, Nickie's brother, was fun, because he let me in on so many secrets.

"Almost all my friends from high school were gay."

I said, "From the old neighborhood?"

"Yeah, from Mott Street in Little Italy."

"Get atta here! All those manly Guido Italians?"

"No, we're talkin about *the sons* of manly Guido Italians. They all were gay. I have ten friends from Mott Street that are all gay."

... and the stories.

"We would be in Carmine's house and if his mother had to go shopping, she would say, C'mon boys, we gotta go shoppin. Grab the shopping bags from the closet!"

Then each of them would grab two shopping bags, ... full.

I said, "She went out with full shopping bags?"

"Yeah, they were full of money."

"Money!"

"Tens of thousands of dollars that she kept in the house. Money they couldn't put in the bank. It wasn't safe anyplace else, so she kept it in the house. Trust me, it was safe in that house. We would march down the street with two shopping bags each. We would go get bread, we would pick up pastries and go to the fish store and to the butcher, ... while carryin forty-thousand dollars with us."

"Why did she have to take the money out?"

"She had to carry the money with her because the money couldn't be left in the house by itself. As long as somebody was in the house, the money was safe."

He was a hell of a nice guy, Carmine. He later became a priest and he had a longtime boyfriend for twenty years.

Another one, Little Louie, had a fetish for nuns. Every Halloween he would dress up as a nun and he would go out like that. This started when he was twelve years old and it lasted until he was about thirty years old. He would hand-make the nun's habit exactly for every religious order.

"Oh, Sisters of Perpetual Help? Oh, they wear such and such ... and in 1947 they changed the habit, and in 1973 they went to another habit. They raised the hem on the habit an inch and a half."

Another one that I knew personally, was Patsy. He used to hang out with me when I was workin at Grant's. He would come into Grant's to get his hair done. He always had bleach blond hair that was a little too long for a boy but short for a girl. He had this round baby face with no hair on it. He was constantly bein mistaken for a girl.

He always carried a big satchel shoulder bag. He would look at women's bags and say, "Oh, how much is that bag over there?"

"That's twenty dollars, ma'am."

"I'm not a ma'am! I'm a sir! Why are you callin me ma'am? I don't believe these people!"

Then he'd walk away with a wiggle and his head up, shakin his head. "I don't understand why they think I'm a girl."

He ended up gettin a full set of breast. He let his hair grow long and he started dressin everyday. His father was very well connected and Patsy was a disgrace to the family. They used to shame him constantly. "Why do you have to do this?

He had to move to Brooklyn because nobody knew him in Brooklyn. They all knew him in Manhattan and Staten Island because that's where the family was. They were a Manhattan family and they were bosses in Manhattan and Staten Island, but not in Brooklyn, so he could get away with more there. He was fully dressing now with the long hair and people wouldn't put two and two together.

But every few months he would have to go to a family wedding.

His father would say, "I'll break your legs you show up like that!"

"Don't you dare show up at that wedding dressed like that, you better show up appropriately. We will kick your ass! You'll have no money to live on, nothin!"

So he would have to go to the hospital, have the implants taken out. He would cut his hair short and grow in a beard.

Every time they would go to one of these weddings, there would be a table set aside for the kids, (even after they were all grown) where Mario and Carmine and Little Louie and all the boys from the neighborhood would sit together.

"Oh, here comes Patsy in his suit!"

He'd be fiddlin with his collar or with his pants. "Ach, God, it's so uncomfortable to dress like a boy! It's disgusting!"

Or he'd have girls' flats on instead of laced up shoes.

"Patsy, look at your shoes!"

"What's wrong with them? They're black, they're flat."

"They're girls' flats!"

"Nobody's gonna know. I can't stand walkin in tie-up shoes with the fat heel. They're so uncomfortable."

Then two days after the wedding he would go back into the hospital, have the implants put back in again, grow his hair long again, shave and dress.

Their fathers were very well connected, and they took very good care of the family. The mothers were treated like the Virgin Mary. They didn't have to want for nothin, all they had to do was cook and clean and take care of the kids. So they doted on the boys. They did everything and anything for them. The son of a made man either does the family business or gets into some kind of a legal business, or he's taken care of, so Patsy was taken care of. They paid his rent, they paid his gas, electric and telephone. Everything. What was he gonna do, get a job as a cook? As a waiter? Bein the way he was, his father much rather take care of him than for him to go work at a job and act the way he was and say who he was.

Patsy was short, tiny, and totally passable. He had a girl's voice on him, and when he started doin the hormones especially, he was totally unreadable. He was Loretta.

Loretta would go shopliftin. He would take all sorts of stuff shopliftin. When they were selling a development of houses, he would go into the model house and he would steal different ashtrays and vases. He was a real kleptomaniac. He would steal everything he could fit in his bag. He always carried this gigunda bag over his shoulder and he would fill it up with anything he liked. Then he would go and sell it. Nothin he needed to do, he just did it for the kicks.

For even more fun and games, he used to put ads in the paper sayin, "Young lady with double D breasts, willing to do massage for the right man."

They would show up expecting a woman and thinking it was a woman. Then he would undress and they would go, "Holy shit, what the fuck is that?"

"Well, don't you like it?"

"Well, it's fine, okay."

Or no. Or they would like it. Whatever.

"I meet nicer guys by puttin an ad in the paper than I do by goin to hang out someplace. If I got into trouble, my family would really be pissed off at me if I got into a fight in a bar and I had to call them to take care of things."

"Patsy, you're really disgracin us! Disgraziato!"

So it's much better they come to my home.

He would order pizzas and he would seduce the pizza delivery guy. Loretta would seduce everybody because he looked like a girl. And he did this prostitution that he really didn't need to do, but he liked to meet guys.

30. DAD'S DEATH

Humans are like the trees and death is like the trees in winter. In the winter they lose their leaves, and the people can see no life in them. They seem to stand alone ignored by others. But that is all an illusion because deep down in the roots there is the warmth of life and far from being alone, there is the communication with the earth and with the other trees. There is the fire of life, just waiting for the Spring. And that is the way that death is in people. We can only see the death and believe that it is all over, but deep down is the soul, the warmth of life, and the fire that is just waiting for the Spring.

The day that my Dad died, my mother called me and said that he refused to take the pain medicine for the cancer in his stomach. No, no, I'm not takin that stuff, it makes me all stupid. My mother said, he's finally decided to take the pain medication. I'll call it in to the St. George pharmacy. Could you pick it up across the street from the salon?

I excused myself from the salon, picked up the medication and I ran home to Boysbarn. I walked in, passed my dad's room and I looked in at him. He was sitting up in bed. He looked at me and he waved and he smiled. I went in to my mother in the living room.

"Here's the medication for him."

"Oh, I'm so glad, he's in so much pain."

"He looks like he's okay. He just waved to me."

"Oh, no. He's in horrible pain. I just came in here because I had to do something else but I've been sittin with him all this time. He's been moaning and gasping for breath."

"He didn't look that bad at all."

"C'mon, come inside," she said.

So we went inside.

He was dead.

She started cryin. I said, "Ma, just do me a favor. Go in the living room, sit down for a couple of minutes and get used to the idea. Let me stay with him and tidy him up a little bit."

I said to him, "We have a lot of shit to talk about. I know you're gone, and I respect that. But we're not finished. We need to talk some more."

We called the doctor and did what we had to do. My sister came up from downstairs and sat with my mother. An hour or so later I went back to the salon to close up. On the way I stopped on the pier in Stapleton, and I sat by the water.

"You know dad, just because you're dead, doesn't let you go of the responsibilities that you have for me. I became so much like you, all the good and all the bad. I ain't lettin you go. You gotta stick with me and you gotta help me through this shit. I understand you're gone and I want you to proceed and go wherever you need to go to learn all the things that you need to learn now that you've passed.

But you have this responsibility to help me along. Just dying is not gonna let you go of that. So stick with me and let's get through this together."

Now, I have nothing but good dreams and good memories about my father. He's not so much my father, he's a very good friend of mine. He counsels me, he consoles me, he's there for me to speak to.

31. SHELLEY

I used to go down to Cheecho's (and then Brazil) all the time and hang out. I was doing hair and there was another hairdresser at Cheecho's named Butchie. The salon that he worked in was owned by a heavyset guy, about twenty-five years old, Albert. Albert was very introverted, chubby, and he wasn't good looking at all. He would stay in a corner, very withdrawn, would only say hello to people that said hello to him first, and never engaged in conversation for very long.

Halloween came along and Butchie decided to dress Albert up in drag. So we all showed up in drag that night at the club and in comes Butchie with this big, buxom, fabulous blonde.

Who's this?

It's Albert, but we're calling him Shelley.

My God, you look fabulous.

Why thank you, darling! Oh I feel fabulous! I love being a girl! This is just wonderful!

She had this conversation going, she was outgoing, she was extroverted, she was bubbles and laughter and conversation the whole night. That was the beginning of Shelley dressing all the time as Shelley. This went on for a year or so, then Shelley decided to get hormones and breasts and to come out in the salon, and dress as Shelley twenty-four seven. She was fabulously happy and she looked gorgeous. Beautiful face, chubby, big tits, big hair. Butchie was fabulous at doing banana curls, Grecian curls, so Shelley always had this head of two pounds of hair, done exquisitely. With her gorgeous makeup, she was a heck of a looker.

The following year we went to the Hollywood Cotillion Terrace in Brooklyn. They used to have a drag ball the night before Thanksgiving every year for twenty years. Long before I started going it was already old hat. Once again, it was all mob. They all got tables, they all laughed at all the drag queens and carried on. It was a fabulous turnout. There was a red carpet outside and people would line up on the streets, because they knew about this all these years, "Oh, tonight's the drag ball, we gotta go down and see all the drag queens!"

You'd have to park in the parking lot and then you'd have to walk the sidewalk red carpet for the whole length of the place where they had it roped off. Drag queens would walk it and carry on and scream and throw pearls. You'd go in and get to your table and you'd sit down. The whole evening, there was this gigantic runway down the entire hall that people would walk. They would announce your name and you would walk the runway, two or three times if you wanted to. This went on all night long, people gettin drunk and carryin on.

Shelley had just gotten her breast implants, so she decided to get up there. She was up there on the runway, *oh the girls are hot with this jacket on!* So she took off her blouse and she was shakin those boobies.

Then maybe a year or so later, she decided to go all the way and have the complete sex change. She paid for the sex change by stripping with a group of strippers. Bayzie's was owned by Ginger M and Maxine. Maxine was a stripper, there were about five lesbian strippers that used to hang out together. They were on the strip circuit, they would do their makeup, like drag queens. They looked gorgeous and they were paid plenty of money.

Shelley said, can you get me in?

Yeah, definitely.

They got Shelley in and she stripped, down to a large G-string. She wasn't very large, she said, but it was a large G-string. She had the tits, and she would strip as a woman. and they believed she was a woman. Most of the real girls were all six-foot anyway and Shelley was a six footer, so it worked out very nicely. Then she tended bar at the Moulin Rouge on Forest Avenue, which was a strip bar. She was a barmaid there.

She got the sex change. She had everything done and six months after that, she got married. He was a beautiful guy but for some reason the marriage didn't last very long. She closed the salon and she went back to college. Nobody heard much from her for about six years. Then we found out that Shelley was an English professor in college!

When I seen Shelley, she looked absolutely stunning, with her hair pulled back in a bun and a little pair of glasses. She had lost a whole lot of weight. She was dressing very college professional, very womanly.

She did very well for herself. She ended up being very influential in the community. She came out all the way in the school and she did a lot for gay rights and gay-straight alliances. She helped a lot of students. People said that they found out about Shelley and then they told her about themselves and Shelley would direct them and make them feel better about themselves. I think Shelley was one of the very first people that stood up and wanted to have a real nine to five job with the respect that was due. She had been making plenty of money stripping and tending bar, but she wanted to be a teacher, she wanted that credibility. And she certainly did get it.

32. LEON PASSES AND MIKE JORGE PASSES THROUGH

After I sold the salon that I bought from Lucille in New Dorp, I was full time in the salon with Leon in St. George. There was a boy that lived in the apartment building across the street. His name was Mike Jorge and he lived with his father and his younger brother. He was a senior in Curtis High School, and he was openly gay. He'd come into the salon for haircuts or to get his hair colored. He was the gay boy around the area, so he felt very comfortable coming in and talking to us about being gay and different things. Then one day I got a phone call from a fostering home in Manhattan. They said that Mike Jorge was there and he wanted them to ask us if we were willing to foster him.

"What's goin on?" I said, "He lives with his father."

He had gone to the guidance counselor at his school one day and said that his father had been ongoing molesting him. Curtis immediately called the police and child welfare.

"You don't understand. Leon and I are a gay couple."

"We have a lot of gay teenagers and we feel that they might as well be in a healthy gay environment. He only needs you to take care of him for a year at most until he finishes high school."

"We really have to think about it."

We ended up doing it. Mike Jorge came to live with us at Boysbarn.

He said, "I don't wanna go to school no more. I hate it."

"Mike, you only have this year to finish up."

"I don't wanna go."

"You have to do somethin. The only thing that we can teach you is to be a hairdresser. So go to hairdressing school. Child Services will pay for it and the money they give us to take care of you, you can live on. You can shampoo in the salon, once you're goin to school, and you'll even get a salary for that."

"Okay, that's good."

About a year and a half after that we found out that Leon was HIV positive. Mike Jorge was working full time in the salon, doing assistant work, blowing hair out, shampooing. But he was adamant that he wanted to be a singer, that he didn't want to be a hairdresser. This was something that he was never gonna do for a living. He was going to be a singer and have a fantastic life.

I said to Mike, "If and when Leon gets sick, I want to be with him to take care of him. So I really need you to take care of the salon, so you need to pay close attention."

'Okay, that's not a problem at all. I would be glad to do that.'

So we both taught him as much as we could. I taught him the running of the business and the chemical work. Leon taught him the styling. Mike wasn't very interested in it, but he did what he could.

A year later, Mike Jorge decided to go down the street to a salon called Babushka. He felt that he was being mistreated, that he was a far better hairdresser and he shouldn't be an assistant any longer. He didn't talk to us about it, he just announced, "I'm goin to Babushka to be a hairdresser."

"Why didn't you come and say somethin, that you wanted to do more? We really didn't think you were ready, and you said you didn't want to be a hairdresser."

"No no, I'm goin. I'm finished."

And he left.

Two months after that, Leon got sick and I realized that it was the beginning of the end. I needed to get my affairs in order enough so that I wouldn't have to be in the salon. At this point Mike Jorge had moved out, so I called him. We sat down and talked and I told him, "I really need you back here."

He made some high demands for a salary. I said all right, so long as you take care of things because I'm not goin back into the salon until Leon's better or Leon isn't any longer."

It was six months that Leon was sick, a long, ongoing thing. He had a fabulous visiting nurse, Donna. She would come everyday to do his vitals, to check on him, and we became very close.

One day she came over. I said he's sleepin.

"Yeah. You know, it's not gonna be that long at all."

"No, he's gonna be fine."

Leon's eyes popped right open, "I'm gonna be fine! I'm totally fine!"

We went into the kitchen, I was makin lunch for us.

She said, "You know, you have to really face up to it. It's not gonna be long. A week, six days, four days."

I'm startin to cry.

And she's crying and I'm stir-fryin.

We sat down and we ate while we were cryin. Later she said, "That was the saltiest stir-fry I ever had, with us cryin over it."

I was taking Leon back and forth to radiation at the hospital in Brooklyn. I told him about a really nice restaurant three or four blocks away, and he said, "Oh it's such a beautiful sunny day, let's go have lunch there."

"All right. I'll go get the car."

"No, there's no reason. We have the wheelchair, just wheel me. It will be nice to go through the streets in the sunlight."

(Which was very odd for Leon at that time, for him allow people to see him vulnerable.)

We got there and they sat us right in the window. Leon was sitting with the window in back of him and the sunlight shining through.

Leon said, "Oh, it's such a beautiful day. If I have to spend six weeks being uncomfortable just for one lunch with you on a day like this, it's so worth while."

"Leon, that's so good for me to hear."

Because it was just three weeks earlier that he was sayin to me, *"Did you get everything ready? I want you to give me the pills to kill me. I can't live like this. I'm in pain and I'm suffering and we decided that this would never happen."*

But I just couldn't do this. Now, this one day him saying to me, *just one day like this is worth it*, gave me permission to not put an end to his suffering.

He slipped in and out of consciousness. He would just sort of go away, get out of his body, like he would go over to the other side to prepare things. My friend Jan would come over and do shiatsu on him and she would work on his body for an hour and he would be in that other place. When the hour was over, she would take her hands off him and he would open his eyes and say, "Thank you, that was so nice."

She would be amazed, "He just comes back! When I'm working on him, I can feel that his energy is not there. But then he opens up those big green eyes and there he is."

The nurse and I were standing over him, sayin we never knew when he was in or out. Then he opened his eyes again and he said, "I'm doin fine. I'm gonna have summer solstice with Robin."

"Okay, Leon."

I whispered to the nurse, so that Leon wouldn't hear, "Robin passed away a few months ago."

But Leon heard. "I know very well that Robin passed away a few months ago. What you don't know is that Robin and I are gonna have summer solstice together."

I talked to Antonia. She said, "It's very obvious that he's ready, and he thinks that summer solstice is a good time to go."

She came over and talked to him and he was very insistent that he and Robin were planning summer solstice together.

"Are you sure you're gonna be with him?"

"Yeah."

"You know Robin is on the other side."

"I know exactly where Robin is. ... and I'll be with him."

This went on for a couple of week before summer solstice. Then the night before summer solstice, the whole coven was in the house. Antonia said to him, "Leon, it's midnight. It's summer solstice."

"Thank goodness. I'm so tired."

I shed a tear and stepped out of the room and said, "No, no, it isn't gonna happen."

I was gonna be Cleopatra, the Queen of Denial. It wasn't gonna happen.

The next day around noon, at summer solstice, we went in. Leon kept slipping down in the bed. We had him propped up on pillows, because his lungs were filling up with liquid and his body was breaking down.

The nurse said, "Nothing is working any longer. It's definitely time."

"No, no, not yet! Another day. Another week."

But he kept slippin down on the pillows. I would go in and call Paul and Vinnie and Nickie in to help me bring him back up on the pillows.

Then something revealed itself to me. All the smoke hit me at once and I understood.

When he went to those places that he went to, where he had people to help him, Robin and Aunt Ralph and all those people that went before that were waiting for him, he said to them, "Look, we gotta get Fred to understand, I gotta go. He's gotta let me go, I don't wanna go without his permission."

That day at the summer solstice, it all came together. Somehow they all tapped into my spirt and gave me a good swift kick in the ass. They said, *Let him go.*

Paul and I brought him up on the pillows and I looked at him and said, *no, it's enough.*

I got into bed with him and I put his head underneath my right arm and I stroked his cheek and said, *That's enough Leon, it's time. ... go.*

He looked up at me, closed his eyes and took a deep breath in and let it out, and he was gone.

I said to Nickie , "Go into the kitchen and don't tell his parents anything, wait five minutes so I can pass him over. Then tell them."

I said my goodbyes to him and after five minutes his parents came in and said their goodbyes.

Somebody called the salon and told them that he passed away. Ten minutes later there were twenty people in the house from the salon. Dr. Rivera showed up, I must have seen eighty people come over that day before they took him away. It was the last time that Leon hosted a party.

The next day was Sunday and I was out in the back yard weeding. Paul was renting a room in the basement at that time and he came down and said, "What are you doing?"

"I'm weeding."

Life has to go on and I'm weeding. I'm crying and weeding and crying and weeding and realizing that life has to go on. Even though there are so many weeds, you gotta do this. That's how I worked it out.

It was a horrible time. People would say that their loved ones were not being fed in the hospital, that the nurses and doctors would put on protective gear and treat them like the plague. But we never experienced anything like that. Everybody at the hospital were so very good to him and to us. Right from the beginning when we went to Public Health, when they told him he was positive, right up to the police that came to pronounce him dead, they were all superbly kind and caring. After it was over, I even wrote a letter to the Advance saying thank you to all the people who took care of us but the newspaper didn't print it.

There was no viewing, no immediate ceremonies and Leon was cremated.

That week I went into the salon to go back to work. The salon was absolutely pathetic. There was no money left in the bank account. Clients were so few and far between. Leon had been doin all the style work, I did all the chemical work and the business part of it. With the both of us not bein there for six months, it was left to Mike Jorge and the hairdresser Nina to take care of the whole place.

Bills hadn't been paid. I said to Mike, "Why didn't you tell me?"

"I knew that you didn't want to be bothered with anything, so I just took care of the basic things."

We were two months behind on the electric. The only thing that was paid was the rent. There were supply bills that were overdue.

"I always pay the supplies when they come in," I said. "But you haven't paid for them for three months! Two thousand in supplies for one company, three thousand for another company. What am I gonna do here?"

Then I realized during the week, "Where are the customers?"

He says, "We did what we could do, but a lot of them didn't want to come back because Leon wasn't here. They went someplace else. As a matter of fact, let me break the news to you, I'm gonna be leavin in a couple of months."

"What?"

"I've decided to open up my own salon, and Nina's comin with me!"

"Oh my God, what does that leave me with? I haven't done a client in months. You've been takin care of the people that stayed, and you'll probably take them with you, along with your own clientele. What does that leave me with?"

"I'm really sorry, but that's what I wanna do."

"Listen. Take this salon. There's no point in me keepin it."

"I really don't have the money to buy this salon. And the furniture isn't what I like and it's just old."

"You helped me pick out this furniture a year ago! It's not old!"

"Yeah, but the place is old. My boyfriend is a contractor and we're gonna do the whole place in Italian tiles and we're gonna own the place together ... No, no, we're goin."

So I said okay.

The only thing I could do was to get Sal to come back to work. He had just come back from Florida and we'd see if we could hold things together. But it was just a matter of time. Sal was also HIV positive and it was two or three months after that that Sal passed away. I seen that there was no hope. I had to just let this go.

I told the landlady, "I know we've been here for ten, twelve years and I've never been late with the rent in all those years, but next month I may not have the rent at all, so it's best that I just leave."

She said, "Okay, I can understand that." *Have a nice life.*

Not even like, stay an extra month and see what happens, or stay until I rent it out ... no. *Leave.*

So I just packed up all the stuff and took all the furniture home and reinvented myself.

33. THE RAVEN HEAD

It was a month after Mike Jorge left the salon and I had Jacqueline working at the desk for me. I would be doing three people the entire day, I would be in there for twelve hours waiting for the three people to come in, realizing that my whole world was coming to an end here. I would close up and drive home, going through the parking lot on Central Avenue, which was very cruisy at the time.

There was this young man with a baseball cap on backwards and stringy black hair hangin down the back. I pulled over and he came over to the car and said, "Do you wanna hang out?"

I said, "What do you wanna do?"

"Whatever you wanna do. I'm here to make money."

"Well, I'm not into that. But if you wanna come and have something to eat, then get in the car. It's cold. We'll go and get Burger King."

He jumped in and we got Burger King, sat in the car and ate. Afterwards, he jumped out and I went home. I would see Jeffrey like that maybe three or four times a week. We would go over and have something to eat. At that point he said, "Come on, I'll take care of you for nothin. You're a nice guy."

"No, it's not about that," I said. Really, I wasn't attracted to him at all. It's just that he was a needy guy and he was alone. And I felt needy and alone. I needed someone to need me. I had been a caretaker for so long with Leon and now he was gone, and I had no one to take care of. It's part of the process.

After a month of hangin out now and then, "Do you need someplace to stay tonight? Come on. It's a Saturday night and the salon is closed tomorrow. Come over to the house and sleep over."

"I really can't," he said. "I gotta make some money. I'm doin crack."

"Here, here's twenty dollars, go get twenty dollars worth of crack. I'll make dinner for you. We'll watch television. So long as you can go to sleep afterwards."

"Yeah, yeah, I can manage it."

He was also in methadone treatment because he was a heroin addict.

"What's the deal here? You're so young to be all these things."

"When I was six or seven years old, my father died in a barroom fight and my mother was a fall down drunk. We would find her in the morning sleepin under the kitchen table in a puddle of piss. My older brother and me, we would have to fend for ourselves."

A guy in the neighborhood, name of Charlie the gimp, that was about twenty-two years old would take us to the movies sometimes, take us out for ice cream. Charlie said to my mother, "I would like to take custody of the kids. You can't take care of them, you're goin from bad to worse. At some point you're gonna end up hurtin them. This is a bad environment."

She hesitated.

"I know them, I really think they're wonderful kids."

She objected.

"If you don't sign them over I'm callin child welfare and you're gonna be in jail."

She signed over custody to the two boys. As soon as he got custody he got rid of the older brother, gave him off to fostering.

And as soon as he was gone, he started playin around with Jeffrey. He was really demented. He would play games with Jeffrey like, I'm gonna blindfold you and you're gonna tell me what's in your mouth.

What's this?

Oh, it's a lollipop.

What's this?

Oh, it's a piece of chicken.

What's this?

I don't know what that is.

"Then I found out what it was."

When Jeffrey was about fourteen years old, Charlie the gimp stopped bothering Jeffrey for sexual favors. He started fostering two other children.

Jeffrey said to him, "You better not be doin with them what you done to me."

"Oh, no, I would never do a thing like that. I'm over that!"

Then Charlie married this woman who slept in the basement. Charlie slept in the master bedroom and the kids had their own bedroom. The woman worked during the day, but Charlie was a musician so he had lots of time daytime to babysit. Then at nighttime he would do his musician stuff and the woman would take care of the children. Jeffrey came home from school one day and he found the two little boys in bed with Charlie watching cartoons. All three of them were naked.

"I told you not to do this shit!"

Jeffrey took the keys for the man's truck, jumped in and he drove it into the house and knocked the front porch down. He jumped out of the car and went into Manhattan.

How does a fifteen year old take care of himself in Manhattan? He started turnin tricks.

"At least now I was doin what I wanted, when I wanted, the way I wanted and I was gettin paid for it. I wasn't bein taken advantage of. It's what I knew, it's what I was taught."

He turned tricks. He was already doin drugs in New Jersey and now he started shootin dope. When he was sixteen they were givin fifteen dollars if you take an HIV test and if you come back for the results of the HIV test they give you another fifteen dollars.

Jeffrey made thirty dollars and Jeffrey was positive. At fifteen years old he was HIV positive.

He gave up all hope. He went to hell with himself. He was livin in abandoned subway stations, sleepin on the streets, in homeless shelters, doin as much drugs as he could, whatever he could get. He became addicted to heroin and he started at the methadone clinic. This way, if he couldn't get the money for heroin he wouldn't be sick. He would do the methadone and he would still get a couple of bags of dope a day and smoke crack and weed all day.

I would say, "Jeffrey, you really need to do more with your life."

"What am I gonna do with my life? I'm HIV positive since I was fifteen years old. I'm twenty-six now, what have I got left? I'm gonna die with a needle in my arm."

"Jeffrey, there's more to you. I would love to see you counseling children that have been in your place. That have been sexually abused, that are HIV positive, that are on drugs."

He held no anger toward his mother or toward the man that molested him. "I understand where Charlie was comin from, because he came from a sexually abusive father. I understand where my mother was comin from, because she couldn't undo what she done, she was an alcoholic. That doesn't make it right, but they were victims just like me."

He moved into the house completely. He was a sweetheart. He was a companion. He was needy. He did his drugs. He swept streets, swept in front of my store and the pizza place, the dry cleaners. They would give him five dollars, ten dollars. He shoveled snow in the wintertime. He would wash your windows for you. He would stand in front of the grocery store, people came out with two or three packages.

"You need help carryin that up the hill?"

They'd give him five dollars or two dollars, whatever it would be. But he always scraped by.

He used to hit up his brother maybe once or twice a week for twenty dollars so he could get somethin goin. I would help him out whenever I could. "Freddie can you do me a favor? I need three more dollars."

He would come in and empty the garbage for me, do whatever he could. We would come home, "Jeffrey, are you okay?"

I'm okay.

I'm not okay.

I need somethin.

I need dope.

I didn't make it to the methadone clinic.

One day he had to go four blocks to Victory Boulevard from the salon to get dope. I said to him, "Come on, I'll drive ya."

"I can't. I can't get in the car. I can't sit down, I'm that sick."

He walked alongside the car as I drove. He was throwing up, sneezing, so doubled over in pain until he got to Victory Boulevard. He walked a half a block to where the dealer was, got his dope, sat in the car and shot it up. Then he was fine, happy just to not be sick.

"It's like having the worst flu you ever had. You're sneezin, you're throwin up, your eyes are waterin. Then the second that stuff goes into your vein, that all diminishes. By the time you pull that needle out you're completely okay. It's like a miracle."

That's what he went through.

"That's how I want to end up my life. With a needle in my arm, dead someplace."

"Jeffrey, you've got more!"

Here I am reading things like Marianne Williamson, *Return to Love, I Love my Body,* ... I'm reading Louise Hay, *A Course in Miracles, Self-Help: The Family,* ... and Jeffrey's got this all down pat! He's so perfectly balanced in the way he thinks, no bitterness, no hatred.

"I don't understand it, you're so wonderful, you need to give this away, you need to write your own fuckin book!"

"Oh, you're crazy, you know."

His mother had gotten help at AA and by then she was clean probably fifteen years. Jeffrey knew she was all right, knew, in fact, that she was an iconic figure in AA, a sponsor of dozens of reformed alcoholics. Yet, Jeffrey had never heard from her during those fifteen years. She was livin on Staten Island, he was livin on Staten Island, his brother was in touch with him but his mother never got in touch with anybody. Then one day his brother called him and said, "Ma got in touch with me and I invited her to my wedding."

The brother was gettin married in a month or two.

I went with Jeffrey to the wedding because I knew his brother now, too. The mother showed up and it was very nice, all that goody goody stuff, they all hugged and kissed and said *I'm sorry*.

She said she really couldn't be around Jeffrey because Jeffrey was part of a scene that she couldn't be involved in because of her need for sobriety. She was okay with her other son as long as he didn't drink, but Jeffrey was a drug user and for her to be around him was too dangerous.

After we were together about a year and a half, the cops caught him with one bag of dope. He got arrested and he got sent to Rikers Island awaiting trial. They wanted to give him nine years for sales of narcotics. One bag of dope, how is that sales?

So I sat down and I wrote a nine page letter of the story that I'm tellin you, and I went to his mother and I had his mother sign it and I had his brother sign it, who was a firefighter in Long Island at the time.

On the day Jeffrey went to court I gave it to the lawyer to give to the judge.

The judge said, "You know, I'm reading this whole thing here, and it's pathetic."

In the letter I wrote that for all the times he'd been arrested for possession of a crack pipe, for ridiculous stuff, never once had he been offered rehabilitation, not one single time. Now, you're lookin at him like he's this big time drug dealer? The boy is sixty pounds underweight, he's HIV positive, he doesn't have an address, he never had a job in his entire life, and you're callin him a drug dealer? If he's a drug dealer, where's all this money? He doesn't have a Mercedes Benz, he doesn't have a bank account, he doesn't have flashy clothes. He doesn't have a pot to piss in or a window to throw it out of, and you want to lock him up for bein a drug dealer for one bag of heroin. It's unfair.

The judge said, "Let's send him to the Get Smart Program in Binghamton, New York."

Get Smart was like boot camp. You weren't allowed to see him for four week after he was in. After a month I went to see him. He had done fantastically. He had gained weight, his eyes sparkled. The inky raven color had come back to his raven hair.

He said to me, "Freddie, you can't believe, every single day, it gets better. I keep gettin stronger and stronger and better and better. My head gets clearer and clearer. First the crack went away in five or ten days, that feeling of crack sickness and fogginess. Then the dope started goin away, me being dope sick and dope dependent. The last thing to go away was the dependency on methadone. That takes a long time to get out of your system. But every day it is so much easier to think. My head is so clear, I can't believe it."

He was there for three or four months and the letters I got from him were fantastic. He came home. He said, "Don't meet me at the train station, I have to go and see the parole officer. I'll come home afterwards."

By now, I was able to see things and feel things about him. I said, somethin is goin on here, somethin strange, somethin I don't understand.

He came home and everything was terrific. He looked wonderful. He called his mom and the next day they went together to an AA meeting. Maybe three or four days later he got a call from his mother, and he went into another room to take it.

"What's goin on?"

"She's gonna meet me."

"Jeffrey, there's something on my mind. Are you seein somebody?"

"Why would you say that? Yeah, who am I gonna see? Who the hell wants me? An ex-convict, a drug addict? Who wants me? I'm a skid!"

(a character from skid row)

"Jeffrey, I got a feelin that you're seein somebody. I got a feelin you're seein the girl that you used to date years ago, Adele from New Jersey."

"Why on earth would I be seein her?"

"Because I got a funny feelin that your mother gave her your address while you were in prison and you made plans to hook up afterwards."

"You're out of your mind!"

"All right. I'm out of my mind but all I'm tryin to do is I'm openin up the door for you. I want to be your friend most of all."

The truth is, I had fallen in love with him. I hadn't even been attracted to him when we first met but now that I seen what he was becoming, I fell in love with him. I seen him becoming who he became, him being fixed, and he was wonderful. I almost felt that the way I couldn't fix Leon, I was fixing him. He was doing it all himself but I was helping him. I was enabling him.

You know, this is a terrible thing to do, but I'm gonna hafta do it.

I took my recording machine and I hooked it up to the telephone. About an hour later the phone rang and it was his mother.

"Jeffrey, here's the telephone."

I clicked the on button for the recorder.

Then when Jeffrey hung up he said, "Well, I'm leavin now."

"All right."

When he left, I rewinded.

"Yeah, ma, things were nice."

She said, "Are we meetin Adele again tonight?"

He said, "Yes, we are."

"Oh, terrific."

"I met her daughter yesterday," he said. "We went to the park."

"Oh, where did you tell Fred you were?"

"I told Fred that I was at another AA meeting. It's really terrific getting back with her this way."

His mother said, "Oh, I'm so glad. You know, the program says that you're a newly recovering addict and you shouldn't be with another newly recovering addict, but I think that you too are so great for each other. It was almost like fate when I met her at a meeting. She said, how's Jeffrey? Jeffrey is at Get Smart, and she says, oh can I have his address."

I was like *I don't fuckin believe what I'm hearing. This is exactly what I told him.*

He came home that night.

"Jeffrey, why didn't you tell me the truth?"

"Get off my back. What are you talkin about?"

"Jeffrey, I set up the recorder. Do you want me to play it back to you? I have the whole recording of you talkin to your mother about how you went to the park with the kid yesterday."

"I don't fuckin believe it! Do I have to put up with this fuckin shit? I'm fuckin leavin!" ... and he walked out the door.

And that was the end of me and Jeffrey.

Six months later, I seen him at the ferry terminal. He was on the phone and I walked over. He hung up the phone and I said, "Jeffrey, how are ya?"

"I'm fine. So just leave me alone."

He started walkin away from me.

I said, "Jeffrey!"

He said, "What?"

"You're still in AA?"

"Yeah."

"You do the enabling thing? Do you do the steps?"

"Yes."

"Did you get to the part about making amends yet? Not for nothin, I was an enabler, and they tell you to stay away from enablers, but I enabled you to stay alive long enough to get help."

He didn't say anything.

I said, "Making amends is like if you have anything to say to me that you're sorry for, like *I'm sorry I led you to believe that I was coming back to be with you when I was writing to her.* I gave you the opportunity to say somethin. But at any rate, that's that."

"Okay."

We parted. We didn't see each other for another year. Then I'm in front of my house, raking up the leaves and I see this couple come walkin down the street. The guy waves to me and I wave back because I can't see nothin. He gets closer and my God, it's Jeffrey.

He walks over and he gives me a hug.

"This is Patricia. This is Freddie. I told you about Freddie, he lives here."

She says, "Yeah."

He says to me, "I'm stayin with her, Patricia has an apartment at the end of the block down by Bay Street in the garden apartments."

"Oh? What happened to Adele?"

"That was something that couldn't possibly have worked out. This is Patricia."

The sweetest, most adorable girl. She was from Ireland, she had the brogue.

"She knows all about you," he said.

"That's really nice. You look like you're happy."

"We're engaged."

"I'm very happy for you."

"To tell you the truth, I wanted to call you to tell you. Next week I start as a guidance counselor for Daytop Rehabilitation. Guess what I'm doin."

"What are you doin?"

"I got my GED while I was away. I started takin college courses, and I'm goin to be doin counseling for children that have been sexually abused and drug addicts."

"I'm so happy ... and impressed!"

"I wanted you to know because that was what you wanted for me and that's how it's gonna turn out."

They ended up gettin married and then they ended up gettin divorced. But Jeffrey is still okay. I talk to him every six months or so on line.

34. REINVENTION

After Leon passed away and Mike Jorge left and Nina left, I had hired Jacqueline. She was a transgender lady that I had met at Lil's Café, the restaurant two doors down from the salon. She said she was out of work and I said, I can't pay very much, but why don't you work here?

"I'm glad for the opportunity to have something to do."

I said, "If something else comes up I wouldn't feel hurt if you have to leave."

She was wonderful to have, she would smile at me knowingly when I'd be sniffling in the corner packing something up or rearranging the shelves that Leon used to rearrange. I'd go into my melancholy state and have a few tears. She'd go, "Do you want me to get coffee?"

"Yeah, that'd be nice."

She'd leave the salon for fifteen or twenty minutes even though it only took two minutes. I'd have a good cry and she'd come back with the coffee for me. If we had four or five customers a day it was nice. If I could pay Jacqueline and get dinner out of it, it was a good day.

At one point I said, "Jacqueline, put an ad in the paper. A lot of men don't want to have waxing done in the salon. Put an ad in the paper that I would work out of the house."

That I would do male hair removal. They don't want to come in to a ladies' salon to have this done.

I had a good friend who did male toupees. He said the same thing: "Men don't want to go into a salon to get a toupee done. They don't want to go into a barber shop to get a toupee done. They don't even want to go into a hair replacement salon to get their toupees done. They want to go into a building to an office on the third floor that says, "A to Z Productions" and that's where you get your hair replacements done."

People are like that with hair removal too.

Jacqueline put an ad in the local paper for me, *Man to man hair removal done in the privacy of my home.*

They would call the salon. Jacqueline would say, "Hair play."

"I'm calling about the hair removal."

... and she would set up an appointment.

A lot of men that came in would say to me, "I'm getting hair removed because I like to cross dress. Do you know anyone that can do make-up?"

"Yeah, I can do your makeup, I can do wigs."

So now and then, here and there, I would do that. Then when we closed down completely, I said to Jacqueline, "Put in the paper that we do male to female cross dressing."

It worked out, and I started gettin customers in that direction.

I had assumed that some of the female customers that I still had in the salon, a dozen or so steady customers from the old days, that they would follow me home when I closed the storefront. So I set up the salon in one of the rooms, to do women from the salon. I think two people came in two months.

This is pathetic. This is the end of the end, so let me pick up the cross dressing ... and it started booming.

Then Veronica came in for a makeover. Ex-Marine with two grown children. Veronica was a cross-dresser that also did computer work. She said, let me get you a computer, you really need a computer.

"Oh no, are you crazy? I could never use a computer."

She convinced me to try it for a month.

She put me on the computer and she wrote this up and gave directions to get to Fair Play, after I changed the name from Hair Play to Fair Play. I got so many hits that at the end of the month, when she said, "Do you want me to take back the computer now?"

I said, "No, absolutely not!"

I probably had thirty new customers this month that came in for makeovers to the tune of a hundred and fifty dollars an hour. This was fantastic, this was a whole new life for me.

"You do my makeovers," Veronica said, "I'll get my clothing and my shoes from you for free and I'll do your website and maintain it for free. I'll come in twice a week and I'll dress myself and I'll sit down and I'll work as your secretary and your website mistress."

"Terrific, that'll work for me."

It was Veronica, another light in my life, that illuminated the path for me. And that's the story of how Hair Play passed away and Fair Play was born.

I made an entirely new set of friends, people to hang out with, ideas, people that didn't know Leon, ... not that they didn't hear me speak about him because I never stopped yapping about him, but they weren't his close friends. We could talk about funny stories, we could talk about good times and the sad times. I could let go of Fred and I could become Rain. That's a psychological thing, when people transition and transgender and cross dress, they have a different part of them. I could let go of that sad part of my life, that loss and I could tap into the new. It got me out again with new people, doing new things, dressing, going to places where no one knew me and I was Rain, I wasn't poor Fred that lost Leon.

It allowed me to reinvent myself completely.

35. THE COURT OFFICER

Bessie worked at the Hudson County Courthouse, a court officer. Six foot two, three hundred pounds easily. He loved to dress in disco times because that was his time. He was probably sixteen or eighteen when high disco was out so he liked these big curly wigs, and disco clothing and disco makeup, neon lips. But this was a big girl and tall, and even taller with the high hair a foot above his head.

One year he wanted to go as a French maid,...

"But I want to go in red vinyl. Can you have it made for me?"

"I can have it made for ya."

It was a red patent leather vinyl French maid uniform with the crinolines that would stick out, a pair of red patent leather knee high platform boots and big curly neon red hair. The crinolines stuck out at least two feet on either side, adding to the hips that were already four foot wide. The man looked like a fire engine! A big fuckin piece o' red vinyl comin straight at ya.

Bessie was married with a couple of children and went out with us every Saturday night. Good party guy, would have four or five or six drinks. He could hold his liquor because he was a big guy and he was a drinker and he never got drunk. He would hide his stuff in the basement in boxes and he would take out whatever he was gonna wear that night and he would hide it in the back of his SUV. Then he would get dressed here at Boysbarn and undress here later and put it all in the car and the next day he would put it back in the boxes.

This one day something happened that he didn't unpack his clothes. He left everything in the SUV and he went off to work with the small car to the courthouse in New Jersey. When he came home from work that night he walked in and said, "Hiya, Hon," and he finds his wife sittin at the kitchen table cryin.

"What's the matter? Are the kids okay?"

"No, no, it's not the kids."

"What's the matter?"

"You son of a bitch, you're cheatin on me!"

"What are you talkin about, I'm cheatin on you."

"I went into the SUV and I opened up the back and I found a wig, I found clothing, I found a bra."

"No, no, I'm not cheatin on you."

"Yes, you are!"

"Honey, honey, honey, sit down, please listen to me. I like to cross dress."

"What are you talkin about?"

"I dress like a woman sometimes, I go out on Saturday nights. When I tell you I'm goin out to card parties and stuff like that with the guys I work with, I really go out cross dressed. We go out for a couple of drinks, four or five of us, cross dressed together."

"You're lyin to me! Don't tell me that bullshit!"

"Honey, come with me, look. Breast forms. Look at the size of the clothing. I'm big."

"Well, I'm big too."

"Yeah, but these are four x's, five x's! They're mine, these are my breast forms, this is my wig. Do you wanna see pictures?"

"No, I don't wanna see pictures! Are you sure? Are you lyin to me?"

"No, I'm tellin you the truth."

"All right. I don't wanna talk about. Do what you gotta do, I believe ya."

Two or three weeks go by and he's havin a makeover by me, we were goin out that night. He gets a phone call.

"Oh, okay, Hon, hold on."

Then he turns to me. "It's my wife. She needs money for the kids because they're goin on a school trip and she forgot to get money off me. I told her to meet me at the convenience store. It's closed this time of night, so I said meet me in the parking lot."

"I don't wanna see you like that."

"Just meet me and I'll give ya the money. You pull up next to me and I'll just stick my hand out the window. Take it and go."

So Bessie goes.

... and Bessie comes back.

He says, "You're never gonna believe this."

"What?"

"I go to meet her, and she says, Look at me.

I looked at her and she says, You know you really look good.

You think so?

Yeah, you really do!

Come into the car, take a look at me really with my clothes, my legs and everything.

She said all right and she got out of her car and got into the SUV.

You know you really look good. I'm actually finding this a turn on!

Do you really, honey?

We ended up havin sex in the truck. It was great!"

Sometimes you find out that people fall in love for the oddest reasons. Many times I tell people, tell your wife about it and many times it works out.

Bessie said, "There she was, she loved it! She had sex with me. She said, this is great!"

After that he would go home like that, he wouldn't change, the kids would be out or at a sleepover and the two of them would have sex until dawn. It was the best sex they ever had. Then she started comin out with us, we would go to cross dressing parties and clubs. They were very happy, and they ended up moving to Las Vegas.

36. TULUM

We were in Mexico, Leon and I, and we were exploring in a jeep in the mangroves and down the dirt roads. We met these people who were collecting money to go in. I said, "Well, what's in there?" but they didn't speak English and we didn't speak Spanish.

There were six or eight cars parked there, and they said it was a quarter to go in for parkin. So we paid a quarter and we got out of the car. There was a trail and these boards laid down for crossing streams and wetlands. We walked through the jungle a bit and after about fifteen minute, we found this hole, sideways in the earth. We looked in and it was a cave with a rock top. Above that was earth and forest. In the center of the cave was an almost round body of water about eighty feet across and in the center of the water was a big flat rock standing about ten feet across.

What do we do, do we jump into this thing? Who knows what's in there? But it was so beckoning.

Leon jumped right in and he said, "It's great! Come on in! It's funny I'm tastin it and it's like fresh water and salt water mixed. You're not gonna find sharks in here because it's a mix."

"All right," I said, and I jumped in and we swam over to the rock and in the center of the rock, someone had built a fire. How they got wood down there I don't know.

"Wow, this is almost ceremonial."

Water cuts into a mountain, and it makes a valley. To think that rain fell and made water, that became a stream, that cut into a rock deeper and deeper and more and more and then great bits of rains and waterfalls came down and they cut deeper and deeper and more and more and then you have this cave. It's only created by rain. It's only rain. Only Rain? Only Water? Only Rain.

We spent the afternoon there and then we walked out to the ocean's edge. There were all these volcanic rocks and the water breaking on them. We spent the rest of the day swimming and sunning nude and we did summer solstice circle there.

We went on to Tulum, to the Temple of the Wind. It was one of the smaller ceremonial places that the Mayans would go to, but it was beautiful. The temple of the Wind overlooks the ocean, and the waves crash against the rocks at the bottom of the temple. There were two sharks in the water chasing each other, playing in the breaking waves. It was a magical place for us.

I said, "When I die this is where I want you to take my ashes."

"Okay, whatever!"

I had my camera and I snapped a picture of Leon with a background of the ocean and all you could see was his head and his green eyes and behind him the sky meeting the ocean.

After Leon passed away his ashes were delivered to his mother. She said that she wanted to give some ashes to Fred.

His father said, "Absolutely not, that's disgraceful! No, his ashes need to be buried at the Russian graveyard in New Jersey."

His mother waited till his father went to work that night and she came over with his ashes. She said, "Open it up, take what you want, and close it up again so that my husband doesn't know."

So I did, and now some of his ashes are buried in the cemetery and some of his ashes are in a vase on the mantle in my bedroom. I took the lion's head medallion that I had bought for Leon in Cozumel, with the opal in its teeth, and I put that in the vase with the ashes. I set aside another pile of ashes, because I wanted to take some to Tulum and sprinkle them there. I asked Kevin and Jeff to come with me to Tulum to spill his ashes by the Temple of the Wind.

You can climb down the temple and there is a certain point where you can just reach the water, a foot and a half from where the waves break. I did a little ceremony for him and I sprinkled the ashes in. Kevin and Jeff said, "We were sure you were gonna go in after him!"

Later that night we went to a place called Captain Lafitte, probably a fifteen minute drive from Tulum. Leon and I used to stay there, very quiet, you had to drive off the main street for about a mile through these mangroves until it opens up to this magnificent Gilligan's Island beach. They have cottages that you can stay in and a main hut where they serve meals. That night we went for a walk on the beach in the moonlight. I was getting emotional.

I said to Kevin and Jeff, "Go on, go on ahead."

I don't really let it out completely, but this time with the moon and Leon's presence with me at that time, I broke down. I screamed and cried and sobbed and threw up on the beach by myself.

When I walked back, they said, "My God, we were about three or four blocks in front of you and we could hear you crying and screaming!"

That was it, just lay it out there, then afterwards, just pack it back in the box and put it away and go on with life.

We went back again to the mangrove with the cave. We had since found out that this was one of the places that the Mayans would come to. They would walk from temple to temple, a walk that would take them a year. The fresh water comes down from the mountains and goes into this cave and flushes down to the ocean, and so here, on the way to Tulum, they would do a purification thing where they would go into that cave and they would swim.

It turned out that since our last visit, the whole area had been made into a water park. They tore everything up, and in the area that we swam in, where the Mayans swam, they blew a hole right through. Now you could go in there and if you swam further down from where we went, there was a narrow stream about four feet wide. If you lay there you would float all the way through this cave and the stream of water would take you all the way down to the ocean. That was the attraction now, you would go and put on a life jacket and float away.

There were so many people that your head was touching the feet of the person in front of you and your feet would be touching the head of the person in back of you. You would float down this winding thing for about fifteen minutes and you would come out in the ocean, where they had it caged off, with rocks so it was more like a lagoon. It was really very sad. There was cotton candy and jet-skis and swimmin with the dolphins that had been captured somewhere half the world away.

Leon, you will never guess what happened to that beautiful secluded place we went to, it's now a water park.

Things change, life goes on and what are you gonna do?

37. DATING SERVICE

So, after Leon passed away, my heart was broken and my pocket was broken. If I had three clients that followed me from the salon I was lucky. The makeovers and the waxings were few and far between. I was making food money. I had maxed out three credit cards in the course of Leon's sickness, paying for food, medicines, anything and everything, probably a hundred and fifty-thousand dollars and now I was working on the last credit card. What do I do now?

I had a twenty-two room home. My mother lived in one room bedridden, and me, in twenty-two rooms. When I bought the place, people had said to me, "Why are you buying a house so big? It's a white elephant. It's useless. It's gonna put you in debt. Later on in life ... "

I said, "You know what, later on in life the house will take care of me."

Well, now it was time for Boysbarn to take care of me.

I didn't know what else to do, but I did know a couple of boys that were hot to trot. They just loved sex. I put an ad in the paper, I said, "Body rubs and scrubs, man to man," and we would take it from there.

I had two boys - men - 23 and 28, they came to work and it done very well, very well indeed.

At that point Annie, my ex-boyfriend's wife, came up with the idea.

"That's great, that's terrific," she said, "I can work there and I can bring guys in. I can do spankings, and I can do bondage. There's good money in that and it's totally legal."

"Really?"

"Yeah, completely. I'll run the ads, and I'll get somebody to work with me and we'll just do bondage and discipline, spankings, role plays, fantasy....."

.....because she was into that. She loved getting spanked by old ladies, it was hysterical. She would go to this old lady out in Jersey City, the lady was over seventy years old and she was skinny.

"C'mon in, honey. I think you've been a bad girl, get over my knee."

Annie would love it.

"Oh she was wonderful, my bottom was so sore!"

.....and it's not against the law.

Her and another friend came in and they worked for me. I put an ad in the papers to get more boys in, body rub technicians wanted. I interviewed a few people. I had a guy that came one day for an interview. He wanted to do the man to man body rubs. I said terrific and he was very good.

Afterwards I asked him, "What do you do now?"

"Well, actually, I'm a police sergeant."

"You're a police sergeant!"

"Yeah, in Brooklyn. But don't worry, it's quite cool."

He was bisexual, and he just wanted a place where he could let his hair down and enjoy himself.

I would never hire anybody that was just doin it for the money, it just wouldn't happen. Very often I would get people that would call and say, "Oh, I see you're lookin for a body rub technician."

They'd come over for the interview and I'd say, "Are you gay?"

And they'd say, "No, but for money I'll..."

No.

You can't have the job.

Thank you very much, but if you're just doing it for the money you're not gonna be good at it. You're not gonna be eloquent, you're not gonna be caring, you're not gonna be considerate.

The same thing with the girls, if the girls were very young, nineteen, twenty years old and they were lookin like they were just lookin for the money.

"I don't give a shit what I gotta do, just as long as I'm gettin paid for it."

No.

No.

It ended up that I had six or eight boys and four to six girls, and I was only open from eleven to eleven. After eleven o'clock at night, it wasn't gonna happen.

They were good times and good people. There was one girl that worked for me, Joanna. She was in the kitchen having coffee. I went in and I said, "Your client came and he's waitin for you in the front room."

"Okay," she finished her coffee and she got up and she fixed her hair a little bit, and she walked into the room. A few minutes later she came back.

"Fred! Fred!"

"What's the matter, is somethin wrong?"

"I don't believe it!"

The two of them are standin there, laughin like hell.

I said, "What's goin on?"

"We used to be engaged! We broke up about three years ago, but we were engaged to be married!".

I said, "You're kidding me! Well, I'll give you your money back...."

"No no no! I'd rather stay, really." He turned to her, "If you don't mind, I'd like to stay."

"I don't mind."

After they were done, he said, "God, I wish I woulda known she woulda been this nice if I woulda paid her then. I woulda just paid her and she woulda been great!"

At one point my mother said to me, "What the hell's goin on upstairs? I hear people comin and goin, walkin around up there."

I told her.

"What? Oh, that's great," she said, "that's terrific. God bless ya," she said. "But you know what, you give me the money to hold, because nobody's gonna suspect an old, crippled lady of having all the money under her mattress."

I said, "Don't worry about it, I'll bring it down to you." And that's what we used to do.

People looked and they said, shame on you. That's a low down thing to do, it's immoral. What a horrible thing to do. But everybody was a consenting adult. The guys that came in as clients were the nicest men you ever wanted to meet. I see them to this day in Home Depot or in a restaurant and they're like how are ya, I remember the old days, it was great!

There's a seedy, shady side that people talk about, "It's in the darkness and its a shame!" But it was nothing like that, at least with us it wasn't. I don't think we ever had anyone that we had to ask to leave or that we had a problem with, no one drunk and disorderly, no one out of line, no one nasty, no one abusive.

People need to be non judgmental. It put me in a situation where I had to think about business day to day. I had to clean the house, I had to do some clients myself. Everybody mixed and mingled nicely. People need to not judge. If you're ever in a situation like that, it's sink or swim. One of the girls that worked for me was thirty-four years old and she was a pole dancer. At thirty-four years old she couldn't make no more money. She was gorgeous, she had a fantastic body and she was still dancing, but she would go home with twenty-five dollars a night and the girl next to her that was nineteen would go home with two thousand a night. So she interviewed for the job and she was a lovely lady bringing up a seventeen year old daughter and she did very well. Older men wanted older women. They didn't want nineteen year olds, they wanted the company of somebody that was older. So I put an ad in the paper and they came.

Antonia had moved away, and she came over to visit about six months into this dating service thing. We went out to dinner together and she said, "So tell me what's going on in your life."

"Mmmmh. I'm kind of embarrassed to tell ya, ... it's definitely taken a different focus than where I was when Leon was alive ..."

Antonia had this intense look on her face. She always reminded me of an owl. She was leaning on her hands, her elbows on the table and she was looking at me trying to figure.

"... It's just taken a whole different turn ... "

Antonia had beautiful green eyes, but when she got mad or excited, when her mood switched, they turned almost amber yellow. Her eyes went yellow.

"Freddie, what are you doin?"

"You know, I'm actually runnin a dating service. I have a couple of girls, a couple of guys workin for me. I put ads in the paper, ... body rubs and scrubs, ... male to male, and I have the girls comin in ... doin spankings."

She just smiled at me and said, "Don't you understand, you're doing exactly what you vowed to do.

"What are you talkin about? You're just tryin to make me feel good."

"When you took your vow as a pagan priest, your vow was,

Send me anybody who needs help that I can help. I can't help you to learn how to spell, I can't teach you math. But I can teach you to love, I can teach you how to be happy, I can teach you how to not have shame in your life, I can teach you how to love yourself. Whoever you send me I will teach. Whoever needs that help, I vow to help."

Antonia continued, "When you said that I said to you, *What are you crazy? Do you have any idea what you're saying? You can't take a vow like that."*

"But I already did, Antonia."

"I know you did. Fred. But that's a lot of stress that you're putting upon yourself... Anybody that comes?"

"You know, Antonia, I really do feel that way. I feel that I can help people in those directions and I want to help as many people as I possibly can. That's my vow as a pagan priest and it's not difficult for me."

This dating service went on for a year and a half. At that point one of the girls had a client who was a very good criminal lawyer and he said, "If you ever need any help, let me know." He said to me, "You're gonna get caught. The first time you're gonna get a slap on the hand, the second time you're gonna get a big, big fine and the third time you'll go to jail. So be aware that this can't go on forever."

I had paid everything off and I had fixed up the house. I didn't want to be greedy. I told everybody that we were gonna phase out the girls because that's the most dangerous part, that's what they go after first. Then we would phase everything else out in a short amount of time. So we stopped taking new clients.

At that point, I was advertising with the local paper on a weekly basis, where it said man to man body rubs and I was doing the crossdressing ads too, which were legal to do. but every once in a while they would put me under massage, and I would call the editor and say I wanted to be under the body rub. if you put me under massage, that says I do massage, and I do not have a license to do massage, I do body rubs and scrubs, facials, I have a cosmetology license, I can't do massage. So I says, I want you to send me a letter that says you made a mistake, and they did. We advertised in New Jersey too and the same thing would happen and I would say I want a letter and put me in the body works section.

Sure enough, one nice spring day, all of a sudden I see two cars stop, one on each side of the street. All the doors fly open and four men run out of each car, running toward the house, one of them with a crowbar. I said what the hell is this all about?

I said, "Excuse me! What's goin on?"

He says, "Police department! Just open up!"

I says, "The door is open, come right in! I'll put on some coffee. What's the problem here?"

"We're here because you're operating a massage parlor without a license."

I said, "No, no. I do body rubs and scrubs. I have papers that explain exactly what I do."

One cop says, "Who's in that room over there?"

I say, "Oh, that's Annie."

He knocks on the door and Annie opens up the door in her bra and panties. She had baby pale skin with freckles and green eyes and long strawberry blonde hair that came down in curls. Angelic looking but with a mouth as foul as foul can be. She looks at the plainclothes cop and says,

"What the fuck do you want?"

"What are you doin in there?"

"I'm givin a guy a fuckin spanking."

"Who else is in there with you?"

"My girlfriend."

"Tell her to come here."

Blaze, her Mexican girlfriend, walks over in a slip.

"What are you doin?"

"I'm givin a guy a spanking."

"We'd like to see the guy."

The guy comes over in his underwear.

"What are you doin?"

"I'm getting a spanking."

"All right, go head. Go back to what you're doin."

And to me: "I'm sorry you're gonna have to come down to the station."

I said, "All right, no problem."

They were very, very nice to me and they took me and they booked me and I had to stay in jail overnight. Me and Bubba in a holding cell. (Bubba was very nice, a perfect gentleman.) I woke up to a peanut butter sandwich that they gave me, then they took me into court. They read what the charges were and released me. I walked out of the courtroom, I had no money on me. I was like what do I do? I have to walk home from Stapleton. All right, I'll walk home.

I was standing at the bus stop, and luckily Leon's brother in law was driving by. He stopped and said, "Freddie, get in the car!"

I got in the car.

He said, "What the hell is going on? Look at the Advance!"

He showed me the Staten Island Advance front page. Fred Gorski, arrested last night. Fifty-seven year old proprietor of an alleged brothel and after hours club.

I had people showing up on the doorstep later that day, in the rain with money in their hand.

"Please, I wanna join the club!"

"There is no club."

"No, no... I'm not a cop."

"I don't care if you're not a cop, there is no club!"

I called up the newspaper and I told them, "I don't know where you've gotten your information, but an after hours club and a brothel? That's very boring. If you send over two photographers and a writer, I'll tell ya what's really goin on, and it will sell a hell of a lot more papers. I do spanking, bondage, discipline. I cross dress men into women. It's a whole lot more interesting than what you made it out to be, but it's not against the law!"

We went to court thirteen times in one year. The lawyer said to me, "I know somebody in the prosecutor's office and they told me that they did something very, very wrong and they just wanna get out of it. Don't stop doing business. Don't even plead guilty to putting the garbage out on the wrong day. Do business, you're not doing anything wrong."

Every time we went in front of the judge, the prosecutor would say, "We're not ready yet to prosecute. We want another month to get all our proof together."

On the thirteenth time, the judge said, "Wait a minute, I have looked at this man thirteen times this year. First of all, you're saying that he was running a massage business without a license. This is a criminal court. I don't do licensing issues, I don't do business issues. I don't know why vice went after the man. Vice is only supposed to be for prostitution, gambling, drugs or alcohol. I've looked at you thirteen times and thirteen times you said you weren't ready. I do believe you're not ready. So unless you can do something right now, I'm dismissing this."

"But Your Honor..."

"Do you have something you can do right now?"

"No, Your Honor."

"Well, it's dismissed."

... and we walked out.

So I was thanking the lawyer outside the courtroom. The prosecutor walked over and she said to me, "Don't you think for one minute that we don't know what you were doing."

"You know something? I know you know exactly what I was doing. But I also know you don't know what the hell you're doing."

And she spun around on her foot and walked away.

What I did, was it wrong? Well, it wasn't right but it wasn't wrong. It was something I had to do to survive. I had to reinvent myself. This gave me a whole new set of friends, people to relate to. Nobody was, Oh I remember the old days, Oh poor Leon, Oh you must miss him terrible. Nobody was like that, because no one knew. Instead, everyday I had to think about feeding people and I had to think about business, cleaning and preparing for the next day. We would close up at eleven o'clock and then I would tidy everything up, watch television, fall asleep tired, wake up in the morning and start again, cook - because I made lunch and dinner for everybody, and there was coffee all during the day. It just kept me so busy that the time passed.

Annie was very into the B&D scene, so we would go in to different fetish clubs and parties in Manhattan. I would cross dress to go there, as a mistress, so I'd be all decked out in leather and boots and it was a lot of fun. I said, you know, I really want to continue with the cross-dressing.

Once a year they had the Black and Blue Ball. It was always on a Wednesday and they wouldn't let you know until Monday where the party was on Wednesday. Two nights before the party you have to call this number on the ticket and they'll tell you the address. They were tryin to keep the general public and the media away. It was ran by about six businesses, like the boutique called Purple Passion, who just sells fetish clothing, rubber, leather, vinyl, maid uniforms, gas masks. Then there's the Baroness who just sells rubber, rubber gowns, rubber shorts, rubber nurse uniforms, rubber nun's habits. They would hire a hall and have a deejay and a fashion show, and exhibitions on body piercing and things you wouldn't believe.

The people in attendance were the real show, though. There were girls with forty-four inch breasts and hips and thirteen inch waists. There were people with corseted skin, where grommets had been pierced into their skin and the skin pulled taught by laces sewn onto the grommets. People were hanging twenty feet in the air from hooks in their shoulder blades or under their pectoral muscles. There was a couple that were pierced like cats. They would put whiskers in their piercings, and they had plastic surgery done to make them look more like cats. They were a hoot.

There were a few rooms off to the side, one was just for spanking, and there'd be people tied up. It was a hands-on thing. In another room, a Colonel Sanders style character stood watch over his partner, a big, voluptuous black lady in a sparkling glass coffin. She was cuffed and clamped hands, ankles and knees, so that she couldn't move. All along the sides of the coffin were holes big enough for passers-by to put their arms through ... to tickle her. People reached in and tickled and she would laugh hysterically. "Ha ha! Oh! Ha! Oh, Stop! Ha ha! No more! Ha ha ha!" and they would continue to tickle.

"Stop! Ha ha! I'm gonna pee! If you don't stop, I'm gonna pee all over myself!"

And she would pee in the coffin.

Another place was Paddles in Manhattan. It was a B&D club where they only served soft drinks and ice cream. I brought a married couple there and they loved it. I sat eating ice cream with the wife, while her husband, Ruby Red, dressed in a naughty nurse uniform, was strapped up against a St. John's Cross with clamps on his scrotum and nipples. We shared a banana split as he got beaten senseless with paddles and crops.

"Hit 'er harder!" the wife said between spoonfuls. "Hit her again!"

It was nice to get out. Nobody knew me. It was a whole different me. The business part of me, the salon, was long over. We had gone into the dating service, that was over. Now we were moving into my next phase. I started getting clothes and wigs, and building up a stock and then when all the girls had left, now I could advertise simply one on one cross-dressing, make-up and hair.

At Halloween I said let me try it and see what happens.

In the classifieds I wrote, *Halloween Dreams by Mistress Rain, mistress of the night. Be transformed into a Halloween dream.* It got the idea in there for B&D with "mistress," but it also got the idea in there for the cross-dressing, but it was Halloween, so it was acceptable for the newspaper.

So people would call and say, "What's this Mistress Rain, has this got something to do with B&D?"

"Well, you can come and talk to us in person. We don't talk on the phone."

"Halloween dreams ... does that mean that you do cross-dressing?"

"Yeah, you can come, we can give you a consultation for a cross-dressing."

People would say, "I'm going to a party, so I really want to look like a woman." Then they'd be like, "I really like this. Can I come back and do this after Halloween?"

That's what broke me into the cross-dressing thing. I'd get all dressed up and people would come in and they would pay a hundred and fifty dollars to spend an hour with Rain. Usually it would be that they wanted to spend time with a cross-dresser to get to know what it was like - simply because they wanted to cross-dress.

Then I would talk to them and they'd say, "I really want to do that."

"I can do that for you, it's a hundred and fifty dollars an hour and I can cross-dress you."

"I'll come in next week for it."

They'd come in the following week and I'd sell them a wig and I'd sell them an outfit. I'd tell them where to go to, the Black and Blue Ball, which was very acceptable for cross-dressers to attend. I'd say, "There's a ball coming up and you can come to it."

"Oh, wonderful!"

They'd buy an outfit from me and they would get a makeover.

I knocked everything down to two girls and two boys working. In the very end all we did was the B&D and the cross-dressing. I said that's enough, it got me out of trouble. The gods were very good to me, they allowed me to see what I needed to do, and they blessed me for the time I needed to do it. It was time to stop all the rest.

38. TURNABOUT IS FAIR PLAY

It's uncomfortable to act, for a man to act like a woman or vice versa. But for me, to go out and act like a lady, it was easy to do because it was in me. The attraction of a woman walking across a room, commanding attention and respect, her head up high, being proud of how she looks and what she's portraying, for me to do that was very easy. It's a difficult thing for people not to do, if you belong there.

You want to walk in like, *Oh I'm enjoying it all, I'm looking around, I'm really having a wonderful time.*

This is what it's all about. It's like getting onstage. Back when I used to perform, as soon as I stepped on stage, I would be big smile, eyes open wide, head up. People would look and they'd go, *Oh, wow, we're having a good time because she's having a good time.* If you don't look like you're having a good time, the audience can't have a good time.

I didn't have a drag name then. I did drag as a female fantasy. *And now we bring to the stage, a female fantasy!* I wanted to be seen as a female impersonator. I wanted to step on a stage, and have people say, look at that beautiful woman! Look at that beautiful woman striptease! She's got nice legs, now she's showin her belly, she's showin her butt, she's showin her arms, she she she she she. And then all of a sudden, I take off the bra and the wig and there's no more she, there's a he there. *Oh my God, isn't that a hoot?* Now I was Fred, a female fantasy.

That female fantasy was something that happened whenever I was working a show, from the dressing room to the stage and back again. As soon as I got back to the dressing room, the makeup would come off, the jeans would go on, the sweatshirt would go on, and I'd be Fred again. The two were never allowed to be together.

Until I did this. Now, with Fair Play, more and more often, I was doing six or eight clients a day that were comin over, and they needed to relate to someone other than Fred, because they all had female names that they related to, that they only used when they were workin their female persona. They would come in, one after the other, and now it wasn't just a matter of two or three hours onstage. I was workin my female persona eight hours a day, seven days a week.

And the name just came to me. I wanted something androgynous. I wanted something elemental. Could I be Earth, Air, Fire, Water? No.

But I could be Rain. Something so soft and so powerful.

People would call up and they wouldn't say, can I speak to Fred. No.

"Can I speak to Rain?"

"Hold on."

"Hi."

"Rain?"

"Yes."

Rain is nourishing to the Earth. I'm nourishing people around me to be more open with their lives. As I'm transitioning people physically into a more beautiful feminine self, I also want to transition their minds, their spirits, their hearts into a place that's more beautiful.

Now they felt more comfortable. My claim to fame is that I am what I sell. I am a crossdresser, you have nothing to feel guilty about or ashamed of. You come to me. You come to me because I am exactly what you want to be. I am Rain.

39. A CAROUSEL OF SELF-AWARENESS: STAYERS AND EVOLVERS

There are all different reasons why people want to crossdress. Some people stay that reason for a lifetime, and some of them evolve to a different place.

Some of them are completely heterosexual. One man comes over with his wife of forty years. She sits and reads a book while I crossdress him. She just wants him to be a happy man and a good husband ... and his crossdressing keeps him a happy man and a good husband. He doesn't cheat on her, there's nothing gay about him, he just loves the idea of crossdressing. He loves to make love with her, ... as a lesbian. He feels like a lesbian with a penis ... if you can imagine such a thing, ... I can.

He likes to be on an equal basis as a partner, which is wonderful for her and for him. Isn't that an even better relationship than the typical male-female relationship, where I'm the male and I play the male role and you're the female and you play the female role and that's the situation and it will always be that way. You'll always be submissive, I'll always be dominant, you'll always be on the bottom, I'll always be on the top, I'll always call for the moment, you'll always submit to the moment ... how boring!

Now think about a man and a woman that can be on an equal level where anybody can call the moves.

They go out, have lunch together as girlfriends, they go shopping together, they go on cruises together, where they spend the whole cruise with him crossdressed.

They'll go as friends or sisters. "We'll be sisters this cruise!" and that's how they'll introduce themselves to people on the cruise. "We'll be girlfriends." "We'll be widows."

They sit at the same dining table every evening with the same ten or twelve other people and spin the tale of their lives, totally comfortable with the stories, since the stories are based on their own lives, just not husband and wife. He is an excellent conversationalist. "Oh, my husband died and then a few months later, hers died too.... So sad. But life goes on." And they will get up and dance together. "Oh, look," the other diners will say. "How sweet." The two widowed sisters dancing together. "They don't even need a man, they have each other!"

They'll have all different outfits, but never not crossdressed. He'll never spend one minute on the ship not crossdressed: bathing suits, shorts, tennis outfits, slacks and sweaters, evening gowns, cocktail dresses, whatever the occasion. They both love it, they love shopping together. Whenever I see them they always say they're still like newlyweds. It was only after him confiding in her and saying, I like to crossdress and her saying, that's weird, but go ahead. "If that's what turns ya on, you're still my husband. I still look at you in the same way, I still feel about you in the same way."

"Now he's a much happier person," she says to me. "He's a much better love maker. If I woulda known that he would be that good crossdressed, I would've suggested it the day we were married. He was good, we had children, it was a nice relationship but after he started crossdressing with me, the relationship was far more exciting. He is far more attentive to me and it is far better sex."

Other people come in and evolve. Very typical is a man that came to me at the age of forty-five. He has been crossdressing since he was in Vietnam. When he crossdressed in Vietnam, he went with women. He would go to a hooker and they would crossdress him and then he would be with the hooker, acting like a lesbian. He came home from Vietnam and he found a woman that he fell in love with and married. He crossdressed in secret around the house when she was at work or away.

He called me when he seen my services. He wanted to come in and help around, doing things for me. He came in and helped with the business and he would crossdress while he was working with me. I would have people come in that were having crossdressings and he would help me dress them and then they would want to spend time with him. He said, yeah, that would be interesting, and he would spend time with them and he enjoyed having sexual relations with them, both of them crossdressed. That evolved into people coming over and saying. "I crossdressed with him. I'd like to meet with him when I'm not crossdressed."

He said, "Well, let's try that, as long as I am crossdressed, I'm comfortable with that."

Then to me he said, "But, I don't know if that makes me gay. When I'm crossdressed, I look at a man and I crave a man, I find men attractive. When I'm not crossdressed, I do not crave a man, I do not find them attractive. If I see a picture of a good looking man, well, that's a good looking man and that's all it is. But when I'm crossdressed, if I see a picture or meet a man and he's undressed, that's a big turn on to me. What does that make me?"

Through the years I've found many customers that have the same thing when they're crossdressed. I said, "I don't know. It's just one of those things."

To put a label on a relationship is a wrong thing to do. To put a label on oneself is a worse thing to do. And when you ask somebody else what do you think about me? That is a terrible thing to do, it's a horrible injustice to yourself.

40. IAN THE CONSTANT

If they're lookin at my website, they should be lookin to crossdress, it's very obvious. But sometimes, people will contact me and say, I'm very curious about my sexuality, and I'm curious about you.

Ian called because he was looking at the website and he seen my picture. Maybe he tapped on the articles about me, maybe he looked at the documentary and it had me crossdressed or not crossdressed. Ian was curious and infatuated and he was curious about his own sexuality ... and he was wondering if I date.

Yeah, I do!

He came over, very nice guy, young, married, good lookin, nice job in law enforcement. We seen each other two or three times. He says, I'm very attracted to you. I don't think I'm gay, but I'm attracted to you.

Then one night I get a telephone call.

"Hello my name is so and so, I'm so and so's wife."

"Who?"

She said his name again and then she said, "I'm not even sure who I'm talkin to. This is Fair Play, right?"

"Yeah, this is Fred."

"Well, my husband goes there."

"If your husband comes here, that's his business. I don't know who you're talkin about."

"Well, let me refresh your memory. He actually came there because your mother had a heart attack and you called 911 and he showed up and took care of your mother. He thought you were a woman and you asked him to please come back over later that night after she went to the hospital because you were "so concerned." He came back to let you know that everything was all right and you seduce him even though you didn't charge him because I know that you're a hooker and that you ... "

"Wait a minute. Stop right there! This is enough is enough! First of all, I'm not a hooker, second of all, my mother never had a heart attack that I called anybody for, third of all, I don't dress like a woman unless I'm being paid to take people out - that's what I do for a living, I crossdress other people and I take them out on the town. So where you're gettin all this shit from, I have no idea."

"Well, my husband told me all this."

"Then your husband is a fuckin liar, or he's makin up a story or you're makin up a story. I don't know which it is, and I don't know who your husband is, so don't bother me anymore."

"No, no, please! Don't hang up the phone. I'm only calling because I wanna find out ... "

... and now, I'm puttin the pieces together in my head, *now I know who this is...*

I said, "I really don't know who you're talkin about. I meet a lot of people. If your husband came here, I didn't seduce him. Believe me, I don't need to seduce anybody. He probably made an offer to me and if I said yes, it wasn't a one way deal."

"Well, I'm just tryin to find out whether he is gay or not. I'm just concerned. If he's gay he shouldn't be with me. He should go and follow his dream and not waste my time cause I'm a young girl with an infant child and I need to move on to a better life. I don't wanna be stuck in a one-way street where I find out fifteen years from now that he's gay and he's gonna leave me and I've wasted all these years."

I said, "I completely sympathize with you and I think you're totally right in the way you feel. You need to confront him and ask him what the deal is. But don't ask me! I can't tell you whether your husband is gay or not. Maybe he just wants to fool around, maybe he's bisexual, maybe he's completely gay but that's for him to tell you, not for me. Most people can't even tell themselves that, let alone somebody else tellin you."

"Well, I'm sorry for botherin you. It won't happen again."

She hung up the phone.

A week after that, Ian calls me.

"Well, I'm glad you called! Your wife called me!"

I told him the issue and he said, "No, I came home one night and we had an argument and I said, this is just not workin between you and me and basically I'm not sure about my sexuality because I met someone ... and I told her. She acted like she was very concerned about my feelings and I opened up to her and I admitted that I fooled around with you. I told her what you do for a living, but she probably put it together in a different format."

"Look, if you want to come clean to her, that's fine. Don't bring me into it, it's not the right thing to do. She told me during the conversation, *if you don't tell me the truth, I'm gonna call the police and have you shut down because I know what you're doin over there.* I'm not doin anything wrong. You need to tell her, because that's a threat. That's totally fucked up."

"Don't worry, I'll talk to her. It'll be okay."

A month later I got another phone call from her. Again, ... "I don't know what's goin on but I think he's gay. What do you think?"

"Listen, I really don't wanna get involved with this. You and he need to talk. Go to a marriage counselor, don't call me. I really don't think we should be talkin about him like this. It doesn't feel comfortable for me, and I don't know why it feels comfortable for you."

But she still kept in touch. It turned out that she was drinkin a lot and doin a lot of prescription drugs. It was a bad situation, she tried to commit suicide a couple of times. She was fucked up before she met him and she was still fucked up. She had the baby and now he was very concerned about the child.

About a year into this, she left him and left the child with him and she went off into a world where she wanted to be, drinkin and druggin. Ian had legal custody of the child and he was raising the boy. His parents would watch the child in the daytime and Ian would take him at nighttime when he came home from work. Maybe two years into that the wife was found dead from an overdose.

The boy is now seven or eight. Now that we know each other for so many years, he still says, "I'm very attracted to you, but I don't know if I'd be comfortable to be with a manly gay man and I don't know if I'd be comfortable bein with a transexual because I like all your working parts. I don't know what I would be comfortable with, but I am enjoying what we're doin."

"So just enjoy it! If it works for me and it works for you."

I could definitely fall in love with him but he only comes over once every two or three months for an hour.

"I think about you constantly," Ian says when I see him. "I want to be with you. I love you."

That's wonderful to hear, but it doesn't fit with the action. Just because someone is throwin confetti in your face doesn't make it a party. Sometimes it just makes it harder for you to see. I'm always tellin him, "Come with me. I'd love to meet the boy. We'll go to Puerto Rico, I'll give you the name of the place I stay in, you book a room, I'll book a room, we'll meet on the beach. Hello, where are you from? Oh, I'm from Staten Island too. That gives us an excuse that we can become friends later on ... "

"Why do we need an excuse?"

"So you can explain to your family, to your friends that the reason why you are hangin out with this strange person, who looks like a woman ... "

"Oh, I wouldn't have to explain. I wouldn't be ashamed of bein with you just the way you are."

So he says.

"Yeah, that's a nice conversation to have, but you have parents, you have a whole straight life, you have a career. You wouldn't be able to bring me into a situation like that and talk about me."

"Yes, I would."

"That all sounds very nice, but I'm also in touch with the real world and I don't think so. I live three blocks from your route to and from work, but yet I see you once every two or three months. You gotta be doin somethin else besides me."

"No, no, only you. You're the only one."

"I'm the only one in these six years?"

"Yeah, you're the only one."

"You know, you're blowin lovely pink smoke up my skirt and I'm enjoyin it but I know it's pink smoke. I know it's not a cloud of happiness."

41. ANNIE THE DRUNK

Are there people who should not cross dress? I can think of maybe one person, Andy Nelson, who would soon turn into Annie the Drunk. He was an odd person, even before it started out. He was a drunk and in a very strange head space. I didn't like the idea of even being involved with him dressing him. We did three or four sessions, then I didn't see him for maybe four years.

Then he came back again. We were havin parties. He came over and I crossdressed him and he went out to the party and he got smashed drunk and sloppy, not nasty to anybody in particular, but generally nasty and foul mouth. He couldn't carry on a conversation without sayin fuck in it forty-four times.

"My fuckin shoe in on my fuckin foot, I fuckin stepped on it, and it fuckin hurts ... "

Oh, my God, you're a horrible foul mouth person, *shut up with the fuck, fuck fuck!* And to be crossdressed, it's worse!

Then he started comin in every weekend because he was goin out to Manhattan and he would come in for a makeover. He bought clothes to go out in. When the makeover was done I was very happy to see him walk out the door.

At one point Rita, who was a steady customer of mine, was waitin for me to do a makeover for her and this guy was here havin his crossdressing. Rita first came in when his wife past away. He was very macho, ex-marine, as a kid always played soldier and dressed like G.I. Joe but he always wanted to crossdress. He had plenty of girlfriends but liked to do this and he found other crossdressers exciting.

He was there in the room and the guy said that when he was a kid he was on the wrestling team at Bitterman Junior High School.

Rita looked and said, "Oh, shit you're Andy Nelson!"

He said, "Yeah."

"I know you, I was on the wrestling team with you!" Rita said. "I'm Tom Manzone!"

"Oh, wow, really?"

After he left, I said to Rita, "That's really funny, that the two of you were on the wrestling team."

A week or two after that, I had a scene coming here where two people wanted to come in and do a BDS&M scene. They wanted to get dressed and be tied up. At the same time Johnny, someone else that comes in now and then, also called me. Johnny liked to be a panty boy and he would put on panties and stockings and he would clean my house for me for free. He would do odd jobs; he was good at carpentry. I said, "Listen, I have a scene goin on here you might be interested in."

Johnny said, "Yeah, I'll come over. I just wanna put something on my face, like a mask so nobody recognizes me."

"Good. It's B&D, so I'll put a rubber mask on your face."

The two others were up there tied up and I put panties and stockings on Johnny and I put the rubber mask on him. He went upstairs, but before he even reached the top of the stairs, he looked over the banister at the two men hanging by their wrists from the ceiling facing each other and he said, "Oh, shit!" and he ran downstairs.

I said, "What happened?"

He said, "I know that guy you have tied up! I know him very well. He's friends of a friend of mine. We went to school together."

"Oh, my God," I said. "Then you must also know my friend Rita!"

"Rita?"

"Yeah, well, I don't want to tell you his real name, but he went to that school and he was on the wrestling team too."

"Really? Well, I gotta go. I'm afraid this guy might recognize me."

When Rita came in the next week, I said, "A funny thing happened. Do you know a guy named Johnny that was on the wrestling team?"

"Oh, that's Johnny Nelson! He's Drunk Annie's brother!"

"No way! You mean to tell me that the two of them are brothers? They crossdress, they come here and they don't know about each other?"

Well, bein that I really didn't care that much for this person, Andy, I had to tell Johnny.

"I gotta tell ya somethin. Do you know that your brother is a crossdresser?"

"You know, he was such a fuckin freak in high school that I wouldn't put anything past him."

"Yeah, well, he's still a freak."

"He's a drunk, he used to get into fights all the time. When we were eighteen we would go to bars together where everybody from high school would hang out. We would go in and he would have a couple of beers and he would be so nasty and insulting to people that they would punch him in the face, drag him outside, kick the shit outta him. Then he'd come back in the bar again all bloodied up, clean himself up, have a couple of more drinks and then insult somebody else and get into another fight. And the boy can't fight! People would say, why don't you stick up for your brother?

I'm not gonna stick up for my brother. He gets himself into these things. He's a fuckin moron, he's a lunatic."

Andy comes in one night, gets a makeover and says, "I'm goin to Thailand to have some plastic surgery done. I wanna get tits and I wanna get my face done."

He comes back with the tits. His face doesn't look very good but he has the tits. I talked to his brother and he said, "He showed up at a family barbecue with a tee shirt on. He had long thin hair and his eyebrows shaved. He introduced himself to everybody with his new name and said, this is the way I'm gonna be from now on. "My name is Annie, and if you don't fuckin like it, too fuckin bad."

They just looked at him and said, yeah, whatever. And they continued on with the barbecue. He got piss-assed drunk and nasty with everybody and they had to tell him to leave, ... as usual.

"Nothing's changed 'cept now he's got tits!"

I haven't seen him in years, but I talk to his brother Johnny who still wears panties, very submissive. He's built, with tattoos, out of a relationship with a woman, divorced, adult daughter, nobody knows much about him but he considers himself to be very feminine, very readable, but I don't see how. Although he's very manly and striking looking as a guy, he sees himself as a sissy-ish boy. He doesn't look very good crossdressed, much like his brother. However, he's got a nicer personality than his brother ... but with those manly features.

I took Drunk Annie to one of the LGBT functions one night. They were havin a dinner dance and there he was in this minidress because he would dress so slutty. The skirt has to be as short as short can be, with fishnet stockings where the garters are showin, low-cut top, big teased up hair, overly made up, a cigarette danglin from his mouth. *Fuckin tawks like dis...* "Gimme a fuckin beer!" He drinks it out of the bottle.

People just look and shake their heads, "WHY?"

He was on line for the buffet and he says, "This fuckin guy in front of me steps back right on my toe. I said, you stepped on my fuckin toe, dude."

"Oh, I'm really sorry."

"I oughta punch him in the fuckin mouth! I got a open toe pump on." Then to the other, "You stepped right on my toe. That fuckin hurts!"

"I'm really sorry."

"He's lucky he didn't put a run in my stocking, or else I woulda really punched him!"

We were sittin at the table with six or eight other crossdressers and friends. My friend Kevin says, "Uh, you need to fix that."

"Fuckin fix what?" he stands up in front of Kevin. "Fuckin fix what?"

"Your skirt."

"What the fuck's wrong with my skirt?"

"No, you need to fix your ... "

"Oh," he says, "my fuckin dick is hangin. So why the fuck don't you say my fuckin dick is hangin?"

... and he stuck his dick back in the panties. "What the fuck do I care? I'm not tryin to fool anybody. I'm a dude in a dress, what the fuck is the difference if my dick falls out?"

"You know, Annie," I said, "that's why you should really wear your skirts a little bit longer."

Kevin said, "Forget it. It's like tryin to teach a pig to sing. You try and try but all you end up doin is wasting your own time ... and annoying the pig."

END

About the Author

Rain Storm (Fred Gorski) is still working at Boysbarn on Fingerboard Road on Staten Island. He can be reached at fairplaytv.com as well as on Facebook. Rain Storm would love to hear from old friends and new, and still loves to date. Life is wonderful, but if its only a nine out of ten, let the party continue!

Also from Ferrandina Press, of related interest: *Nickel Fare*, a novel, by the editor of *Making Rain*, Dominic Ambrose.

The year is 1971 and Nicangelo has just turned 21. Though he is still shy and inexperienced in the world, he is a free spirit, out of the closet and living within the context of the hippie movement of his generation. But that comfortable little world is falling apart under the social pressures of the new decade and Nicangelo finds himself adrift in the city, homeless and without any clear directions or resources. He is helped by an elderly drag queen named Minette, who sends him out on the most humane hustling job she could come up with, but that falls through, and soon he is drawn into a darker, more violent world of sexual exploitation and drug abuse. From there, at the bottom of the food chain, he must find his way back up, on his feet and moving forward. His is a pilgrim's progress through the sometimes cynical, sometimes nurturing gay lifestyle of the 1970s, and his only guide is his own perception of a feeble light up ahead.

Praise for *Nickel Fare*:

"Ambrose's gorgeous slice of life is rendered with such detailed devotion and inner accuracy that it comes out as though brand new."
                    Felice Picano, Lambda Pioneer Award winner

"Nicangelo's odyssey reveals a whole world to the reader. It is more sordid (in a good way) that John Rechy's *City of Night* but has a truth and honesty all its own."
                    Arnie Kantrowitz, author of Under the Rainbow

Available at discerning bookstores and at Amazon online. Find more information about this and other books by Ferrandina Press at ferrandinapress.wordpress.com or on Facebook.

www.ingramcontent.com/pod-product-compliance
Lightning Source LLC
Chambersburg PA
CBHW020109020526
44112CB00033B/1109